TO HIDE
THE TRUTH

Susan Noe Harmon

Little Creek Books

A division of *Mountain Girl Press*
Bristol, VA

Little Creek Books,
a division of Mountain Girl Press
Bristol, VA

TO HIDE THE TRUTH

Published November 2009

Although the events of this story are true, some of the names
are changed out of respect for those family members still
living. The time line is adjusted for story continuity.

Cover art by Gainor Roberts
www.gainorroberts.biz

You may contact the publisher at:
Little Creek Books, a division of Mountain Girl Press
P.O. Box 17013
Bristol, VA 24209-7013
E-mail: littlecreekbooks@mountaingirlpress.com

ISBN: 978-0-9767793-8-4

"Susan Noe Harmon is a born story teller at her best in TO HIDE THE TRUTH, a tale of her terrorized childhood and its aftermath. It is a story of growing up amid violence and alcoholism, but together with the horrors of her childhood are recollections of small-town Kentucky, complete with the sounds and smells and sights that bring smiles as well as tears. Artfully shaped, TO HIDE THE TRUTH works its way to the truth Harmon never expected. A moving and well-written memoir."

Edward M. Cifelli, Biographer, Book reviewer, and Memoir writer

"Susan Harmon has written a chilling account of growing up in the 1950s in a household plagued by domestic abuse. This memoir of domestic violence, as seen through the eyes of a child, takes place in the isolated "hollers" of Eastern Kentucky. Unfortunately, at that time, women and children had little hope of escaping the violence. The struggle to end violence against women and children has come a long way since then but we still have far to go. TO HIDE THE TRUTH helps the reader understand why women stay with their abuser—with reasons ranging from love and hope to fearing for their lives. While her mother had "to hide the truth" about the abuse she endured, Harmon shines a spotlight on it in hopes of helping others who continue to struggle in secret."

Sharon Currens, Executive Director Kentucky Domestic Violence Association

"Susan Noe Harmon's words make your heart ache for a child who is growing up in the home of an abusive, alcoholic father. Though the novel presents a raw telling of the main character's experiences, readers will marvel at the girl's ability to find moments of hope and joy in the midst of a chaotic life. This is a tale of survival! Many readers will thank Susan Noe Harmon for her honest depiction of an all-too-common tragedy."

Lisa Hall, Author

"I found it difficult to put down this well written chronicle of one woman's heroic journey to understand the terrors of her childhood as she witnessed the daily ravages of her father's alcoholism upon her innocent mother."

Betty Xander, Award Winning Actor and Director,
Source Theatre Company, Washington, D.C.

Foreword

"Truth is not only violated by falsehood;
it may be equally outraged by silence."
—Henri-Frédéric Amiel

In TO HIDE THE TRUTH, Susan Noe Harmon allows truth to rage against—and overcome—silence, the silence that enables oppression.

"As soon as I began to talk, I learned to hide the truth," begins nine-year-old Susan, a child growing up in 1950s Kentucky. What follows is a harrowing story of secret substance abuse and domestic violence. The gritty tale is tempered by the narrative voice of the child, one of love and concern for her mother.

Susan spends her childhood seeking the intervention of the adults around her and the intervention of God. Harmon presents a plaintive picture of a girl whose life experiences leave her with more questions than answers. Throughout it all, silence plays a vital role.

Mother and daughter spend years tiptoeing around drunken father, fearful that the slightest noise will send him into a rage. Outside the home, both are silent about the nightly torment they endure. Even the expression of Susan's prayers is silent. Yet it's silence that sustains their suffering. Cultural taboos regarding domestic violence and alcoholism prevailed at the time. One didn't air the family's dirty laundry.

Although she escapes the secret violence as an adult, Susan struggles with crippling emotions. She resents her mother for having her hide the truth and allowing them to remain in their terrible situation. She resents her father for failing to acknowledge the personal hell he created for the family. It takes a lifetime for her to overcome these feelings. Only after she sits down with her aged and ailing father does she finally discover some truths about him. "It proved to be the most important conversation with my father I ever had," she writes. He "seemed to survive by placing a positive spin on the most tragic circumstances and avoiding a painful past."

Her father followed the old French proverb that says when one's hand is full of truth it is not always wise to open it. Through this book, however, Harmon unclenches her own fists and reveals her painful past. By doing so, she renounces silence and sets herself free.

Neva Jean Bryan
Author of *St. Peter's Monsters*
www.nevabryan.com

A Note from the Author

For years, I literally wrote this story in my head, never imagining that I would ever put pen to paper on the subject of domestic abuse and alcoholism. With my parents' conditional approval, I delved into this memoir. Realizing that few people were aware of the violence and destruction I had witnessed as a child, I accepted the possibility of raised eyebrows.

As the chapters formed the story, I became cognizant that it wasn't just one factor that created the horror in my little home in the Appalachian Mountains, but a multitude of reasons. The decaying family unit carried the burden for decades, muted not only by the victims, but society as a whole. During those years, to seek help was not an option, and to break family ties suggested disgrace and failure.

My life is different but not unique. Although the events are true, some of the names are changed out of respect for those family members still living. The time line is adjusted for story continuity. This personal story is for the afflicted, those who battle this disease daily, and for the affected, the innocent ones who struggle with the devastation.

Fortunately, the stigma has waned and there is help available to those who want to break the cycle. A page of hotlines and Web sites is included in the back of this book. It is my wish that TO HIDE THE TRUTH will open a door, pose a question, or start a dialogue; a positive change begins with one small step.

Susan Noe Harmon

Dedication

My memoir is dedicated to the victims, the innocent ones who suffer from the devastation of domestic abuse, that they may seek a better way of life. This story is also dedicated to those who struggle with the demons of alcoholism, that they may choose a path of healing and recovery.

CHAPTER ONE

As soon as I began to talk, I learned to hide the truth. My mother told me, "Honey, it really isn't a sin, we're just keeping secrets." In 1958, I turned nine years old. Until then, I had no thoughts about my life or anyone else's. Mama still looked the same, Daddy still acted the same, but I kept changing.

By midmorning, the Kentucky August sun beat down on my head, making my hair drippy wet. I sat in the front yard digging around in a clover patch, in search of a four-leaf clover to bring me some good luck. A sweat bee zoomed in front of my face while I ran my fingers through the green tuft. It fell dead when I clapped it between my hands. I wasn't afraid of its bite, but I've been known to cry from a single honeybee sting. I grabbed a cluster of dried dandelions, blowing the tiny white cotton balls into the air. I soon gave up on the four leaf clovers, and picked some scattered wild violets to give to Mama. A hot breeze shook the tree leaves. Looking toward the mountain ridge, dark clouds rolled, a preview of a summer rain. I wasn't afraid of lightening and thunder, only the storm brewing inside my house.

Mama opened the screen door. She had worked all day, washing and waxing, sweeping and polishing. She cleaned house on Saturdays; I always tried to stay out of her way. "Susan, time to come in. Lunch's ready," Mama said. "Then you can help me hang the wash out on the clothesline."

Before I spouted words of the impending rain, a boom of thunder rattled the windows. I jumped up and ran inside. We took refuge in the living room, both of us sitting on the faded gray couch as the bursts of lightening blinded our eyes like the flashbulb of a camera.

"Hurry, pull your feet up on the couch!" Mama hollered. "The lightning's dancing on the floor."

I did as I was told. Sure enough, it looked like little sparks of electricity jumping to and fro on the hardwood floors. I never questioned my mother about worldly matters because she knew everything.

The shower left quickly, scarcely dampening the blades of grass. I ate lunch as Mama gathered the wet clothes out of the wringer washer into a laundry basket. She got a clean rag out of the pantry to wipe the clothesline of any dirt, rain, or bird droppings. The kitchen reeked of bleach. I figured that Mama spent a lot of money on Clorox because she used it on everything. She even talked Granny into soaking her false teeth overnight in Clorox water. The year earlier, my cotton underwear turned pink when she accidently left a red bandana in the washer with the white clothes soaking in bleach water. At the time, she told me it was the new style. I didn't care.

As I pulled the wet clothes out of the basket and shook them, Mama grabbed two wooden clothes pins. Holding one in her mouth, she used the other one to fasten the clothes to the clothes wire. She clipped the second pin to join another piece of clothing so that no space on the wire was wasted. We worked like a team.

"Mama, do you think Daddy'll be home late tonight?" I asked, handing her one of my father's shirts.

"I don't know, Susan," Mama replied, not looking directly at me. "Why?"

I couldn't think of what to say next. I felt like I was going to burst inside, yet, I knew to keep quiet. "I was just wondering," I said, softly.

After my job was done, I sat on the edge of the planked front porch. I picked up my wilted forgotten violets, scattering them about in the yard. I watched two robins flitter in the maple tree next to the house. Looking closer I saw their nest, made of twigs and leaves. The daddy robin flew off after chirping loudly. I climbed up in the tree, and leaned over for a closer look. The mama robin flapped her wings, giving me a fright. I nearly fell as I raced down the trunk of the maple. I ran behind the house for fear the bird might chase me. Out of breath, I squatted down next to the chimney, not realizing I stood in coal soot. With my shoes now covered, I knew I would catch the devil if I walked in the house tracking black. Quickly, I took them off in the grass, rubbing them hard against damp blades. It worked.

With Mama busy ironing the sheets and towels, I sneaked off to the nearby playground. Disappointed in finding no one to play with, I twisted around in a swing, knotting up the links, then letting go, spinning like a top. When I tried to walk, I staggered; my head feeling woozy. I wondered if Daddy ever felt that way when he was drunk. I sat down on the curb next to a stop sign and watched a mother mouse crawl out of the sewer grate with three little babies trailing behind. I wanted badly to stroke them in my hand, to take them home. But, I remembered what Mama did the last time I brought baby mice home. She grabbed them all at once, and threw them into the blazing furnace. There was no telling what she would do since it was summertime. She dared me to ever touch a mouse again, lest I contract a disease and die.

The day was long; the night would be longer. Mama simmered a pot of pinto beans on the stove for hours, fried potatoes in bacon grease, and baked a skillet of golden cornbread for supper. The sliced tomato and the onion from Granny's garden were decorations for our fine meal. I ate heartily as the sun beamed afternoon shadows throughout the house. With the windows and doors open to stir the air, I imagined folks passing

3

by wondered whose house kept such mouth-watering foods. Mama ate very little. We didn't talk.

At eight o'clock, I didn't complain when Mama ran my bath water. She only allowed three inches of water in the claw bathtub for washing body and hair. I never questioned her, but often wondered what would happen if I bathed in five inches of water. I promised myself that when I grew up, my bathtub would hold a full six inches of water every time.

I sat on the couch in my thin, cotton, shortie pajamas, the ones from Aunt Grace. Mama's sister brought a sack of old clothes when she visited Granny earlier. Rummaging through the hand-me-downs was always more exciting than getting store bought clothes. Aunt Grace's old clothes were soft and broke in; unlike the store bought clothes, stiff and cold.

The reception on our black and white television became fuzzy. The week before, Mama climbed up in a tree outside the window to hang the antenna on a branch for better reception. Sometimes, especially after a heavy rain, the picture rolled like a tin can.

Mama stared at the television program as she often did, with no emotion. I studied her face, her sad eyes, her pale skin. I watched as her body trembled, about the same time every evening. I wished she could stop shaking. I hated that. On the end table beside her little chair, the ashtray overflowed with cigarette butts. Her coffee cup empty, she finished the second pot of coffee since noon. At nine-thirty, she took the ashtray and cup into the kitchen. Time was near.

"Mama, I think I'll go to bed," I said, standing in the kitchen doorway watching her peer out the kitchen window into the darkness.

"Sure, honey, I'll be in to kiss you goodnight in just a minute," she answered, not taking her eyes away from the black of night.

In my little room, I knelt beside my twin bed, and recited my prayers. After climbing between the freshly bleached sheets,

I pulled my cover up to my neck, even though the night air through my window was sticky and humid. I felt protected.

Mama came in, closed my window, and turned off my bedroom lamp. She sat down on the side of my bed. "Did you say your prayers?" she asked, stroking my hair away from my face.

"Yes, I did. Mama, it's so hot in here. Can't I have the window open just a little to catch a breeze?" I begged, already feeling the bed sheet damp from my body heat.

"Honey, you know we have to shut the windows. It's not all that hot in here. I'll get the floor fan, and turn it in your direction. Now, you go to sleep as quickly as you can. I love you," she said, and kissed me goodnight.

"I love you, too. Mama, don't shut my door," I pleaded.

"Don't worry, Susan. It won't close anyway," Mama answered, while she set the floor fan blowing hot air into my room.

The lights from the kitchen and living room shed enough light into my bedroom so that I could see everything in my room. On my wooden desk sat: a lamp, a half-finished coloring book, three crayons, a Sheaffer fountain pen, and a deck of Old Maid cards. My Tiny Tears doll sat in the little woven rocker that I used as a baby. Along one wall, Mama nailed some boards for a bookshelf. She thought it was important for me to read real books, she called it, besides my funny books. I enjoyed *The Wizard of Oz*, wishing many times to be swooped away forever. I rolled on my side, focusing on my paint-by-number dog picture on the wall next to my bed. It took me all winter to paint it. Although pleased, I concluded that would be the first and the last one.

Taking a deep breath, I began my ritual of reciting nearly every prayer I ever learned. Curled up in a fetal position, I squeezed my prayerful hands so tight I lost feeling in them when I finally unclasped. My stomach churned, hot water rose in my throat, burning, acrid. I swallowed and coughed. I held my breath to pray. I crossed my fingers and my toes, wishing time would either flash or just stand still at that very moment. I heard Mama in the kitchen, stirring about, sobbing.

In my half asleep, hyperalert daze, I heard a car door slam outside around midnight. With shallow breaths, I counted numbers as if counting his steps until he opened the front door. A living room light showed his shadow as he stomped through the house, stopping at the kitchen doorway. His words began low and jumbled; I couldn't hear my mother's voice. Within minutes, his voice roared, damning Mama to the fires of hell and everywhere else he could think of. I heard a glass break, and a chair thrown. I wrapped my arms around myself and squeezed tight, as if preparing for a great wrath. Mama screamed as I heard a sharp smack. Feet shuffled on the linoleum. Then, quiet. Did he kill her? I jumped out of bed, and ran into the kitchen, finding Daddy's massive hands around Mama's throat, his eyes blazed in anger. Mama's mouth hung open, her eyes bulged, a trickle of blood oozed from her nose. I pulled hard on Daddy's arms.

"Daddy, stop it! Stop it! You're going to kill her!" I screamed to the top of my lungs, beating him with my knotted fists. "Daddy! Let Mama go!"

Daddy suddenly loosened his death grip, and looked at me. Mama slumped to the floor. I helped her into a kitchen chair.

"I'm going to bed," Daddy announced royally. "I love you, Susan."

"I love you, too, Daddy," I uttered, watching him stagger into the bedroom.

I turned to my mother, seeing a half-dead woman propped up, gasping for dear life. I cradled her head gently. "Mama, are you all right?" I whispered. "Do you want me to call the doctor?"

"I'm okay. Don't dare call the doctor. I'm fine," she choked, wiping her nose.

I picked up the clumps of Mama's hair freshly yanked out of her head and put it in the garbage. I wondered how long would it take to pull her bald. I took the half empty bottle of Kentucky whiskey and hid it in a cabinet underneath the kitchen sink. After helping Mama to the living room couch, I gave her my pillow to sleep on. It was 4:00 a.m., soon to be daylight. I laid down in my bed and closed my eyes.

Too soon the fiery sun burst through my window, calling for me to get up. I raised my window to hear the chirps of the birds, and the business of nature on a Sunday morning.

"Susan, get up. It's time to get dressed for church," Mama hollered from the kitchen. "Get up, sleepyhead!"

I went into the kitchen to see Mama already dressed in her green church dress, a scarf wrapped around her neck, her hair styled differently, and a smile on her lips. Daddy came out of the bathroom dressed neatly in a white starched shirt, creased brown pants, and spit-shined shoes. Instead of reeking of liquor, he smelled fresh-shaven with Old Spice.

"Good morning, honey!" Daddy said, sweetly.

I answered robot-like. Although hungry, I wasn't allowed to eat if I was to take Communion. I still felt a knot in my stomach from hours earlier. Finding my blue print dress in my closet, I quickly dressed, combed my straight dark hair, and put on my best Sunday shoes. Actually, I had one pair of church shoes, but they were my favorite.

Daddy drove us to the little Catholic church less than ten miles away. With Mama sitting in the passenger seat, I sat in the middle, between Daddy and Mama. That was my place in the car, and the family.

The little brick missionary church was nearly full when we arrived. Mama and I put our small round veils on our heads with bobbie pins before entering the vestibule. Daddy stood impatiently behind us. We walked inside, made the sign of the cross with holy water, and took our seat. As the Latin Mass slowly moved along, I turned my thoughts to last night. I didn't realize my breathing was hard until Mama leaned over, asking me if something was wrong. Mama, Daddy, and I took Communion together, as expected of a family dedicated to the Catholic faith. After services, Daddy stood outside on the steps with a small crowd of men, their voices loud with laughter. Still inside, Mama lit a candle in front of the statue of Mary, and knelt down in prayer. I never asked her what she prayed for. I guess I already knew.

Daddy dropped me and Mama off at the house, saying he would be back later. We knew where he was going. I only wished he would stay there. The local bootlegger had most of his barbering wages every week anyway.

Mama and I changed out of our Sunday clothes, hanging up our dresses to be worn again next Sunday. Gently, Mama took her scarf off of her neck.

The smell of fried chicken nearly tortured my insides as I watched Mama turn the pieces in the iron skillet heavy with shortening. A kettle of greasy beans, cooked in a slab of fatback with little white potatoes on top, made my mouth water. I wished she enjoyed eating as much as I did.

"Mama, why don't we have a picnic in the back yard? I can get the old quilt and spread it out over the grass," I said. "It'd be fun."

She turned painfully to look at me with her sad eyes. "Sure, we can eat outside. Go on now, and get that ragged quilt out of the closet in my bedroom. It'll be ready in a few minutes. We'll fill our plates in here, and take them outside. You get the silverware, too," Mama said.

I tried not to notice the purple marks on her neck. I figured it must hurt a lot, but I didn't say anything. I found the ragged quilt, folded neatly in the back of the closet. Underneath the quilt was an old shoe box that captured my curiosity. It was tied with kite string. I loosened the knot, raised the lid, and peeked inside. To my surprise, a silver gun shone with white tissue paper around it. I counted three bullets.

"Susan, did you find the quilt? Dinner's ready. I'm waiting," Mama hollered.

I jumped, catching my breath like a hiccup. Quickly, I closed the lid and tightened the knot. Grabbing the quilt, I ran out the back door and spread it on the grassy lawn under one of the maple trees. After filling our plates, we sat in the shade, just the two of us. I noticed Mama eating a bit more than usual. That pleased me.

"Are you excited about school starting in a couple of weeks? You know, fourth grade is very important. Sister Mary told me after Mass that you were a very bright student. She thinks you'll do just fine in math this year," Mama said. "I know it's your hardest subject."

"I heard that fourth grade means long division. I sure hope I can remember all the multiplication tables. I just hate arithmetic. It never comes out like it's supposed to," I complained.

"Don't worry. Maybe I can help you. If I can't, maybe Daddy can," Mama suggested.

"No, Mama, I don't want Daddy to help me. Just you!" I insisted, my eyes fixed on her bruised neck.

We finished our meal in the quiet, with an occasional tweet from a robin's nest nearby. I gathered the plates, glasses, and silverware, while Mama shook the quilt. Inside the house, I washed the dirty dishes as Mama dried and returned them to the cabinet. She wrapped a full plate of food for Daddy, for whenever he came home.

Sundays seemed to have more hours in the day. It was difficult to find something to occupy my time, something to keep my mind away from anticipating the darkness. We watched television until I couldn't sit still any longer. I played hop scotch on the sidewalk until a couple of older kids walked by, smudging my chalk lines on purpose, laughing at me. I spent time jumping rope until I was out of breath.

Finally, the sun dropped behind the mountain, giving way to a coolness for the evening. I was tired of waiting. I wanted to get it over with so another day would come.

After Mama tucked me into bed, she read *Thumbelina* to me from my fairytale book. I knew it by heart, but it always seemed special when my mother read it to me. Before she turned out my light, she kissed my forehead with love.

Sometime after midnight, I heard Daddy open the front door, slamming it hard, rattling the windows. Mama was in bed. Finding the plate of food, Daddy sat at the kitchen table, ranting and raving between bites of chicken. Cursing the air, threatening to burn the house down, he yelled for Mama to pour him a glass of milk which she did; she had no choice. She kept out of his reach, running into the living room as he tried to grab her. I stayed in my bed, thinking she would be okay as long as I heard noise.

After he ate, he bounded into the living room, flailing his arms, screaming. Mama ran out the front door to hide in the dark. Daddy locked the door. He peeked in my room, only to find me faking sound asleep. Then, he went to bed. When I heard him snoring, I got up, unlocked the door, and motioned for Mama to come inside. This time, she crawled into my bed with me. We didn't speak; we didn't have to.

The next morning, I woke to the smell of fried bacon. I hurried into the kitchen. "It sure looks good, Mama," I said, sitting down to a plate of bacon and scrambled eggs. I tried to eat, but the knot in my stomach kept forcing the food up in my throat, burning.

Mama didn't notice. She went into the bathroom to finish getting dressed for work. I ate a few bites. Then, I emptied the plate into the garbage so she wouldn't worry. Daddy was still in the bed. I got dressed in silence, wearing some of my aunt's sack clothes. The shorts and shirt smelled like mothballs: I didn't mind.

Mama took me to Granny's house for the day. I kept my eyes on Mama's face, studying the worry lines around her eyes and her forehead. I thought she was still pretty, even when Daddy beat on her. Another delicate scarf covered her slender neck.

"Now, Susan, don't say anything to Granny about Daddy," Mama reminded. "We don't want to worry her. And, besides, it's kept in our house."

"I won't," I promised.

During the summer months, I stayed at my grandmother's house while Mama worked. Granny raised chickens, selling eggs and an occasional fryer chicken. In my Granny's yard, there was a rusty swing set with a teeter-totter that rattled and made scraping sounds when pushed. I spent the day outside playing, digging in the dirt, and making chain necklaces from clover flowers. Granny kept busy with her chickens and her garden, unaware of the secrets stirring about. Most of my friends were imaginary, simply because it was easier for me to play with them than to play with a real person. I did have Blue, my little chicken that Mama bought for me that Easter. I raised it at home until it was too big; then, we brought it to Granny's where she kept it in the yard for me.

Mama's job was at an insurance company in town. She never took a sick day, even when she got sick. She never took a vacation, although there was no place to go, anyway. I think her work was her salvation. Since Daddy spent all his money on whiskey, Mama worked to pay the bills.

By the time Mama stopped to pick me up, Granny had supper on the table waiting. I listened as Mama and Granny talked about me going to school after Labor Day. They planned my clothes, shoes, school supplies, lunches, and my life. It was as if I was the invisible third person sitting at the table. I didn't really mind. It was good that Mama had a mother to talk to.

On our way home, I noticed Mama driving slower than usual. She gripped the steering wheel with both hands, her knuckles ghostly white. As we started on Moo Cow curve, she turned the steering wheel as the road rounded between the mountainside and the Cumberland River. Suddenly, she failed to straighten the tires according to the road. The car was heading toward the river! Mama's head slumped down, her eyes closed, her hands still on the wheel. I screamed, and grabbed the steering wheel, turning it in the direction of the mountainside.

"Mama! Mama! Wake up!" I screamed, still trying to steer the car down the two lane road. "Oh, God, help me!"

Startled, Mama jerked her head up. By that time, we were in front of Mike's Drive-In. She pulled off to the side of the road and stopped the car. She burst into tears.

"Mama, it's all right," I cried, cradling her head on my shoulder. "You must've fallen asleep. We can sit here a minute."

The carhop started toward the car, but I waved her off. Mama wiped her eyes, her hands shaking.

"I'm so sorry, Susan," Mama sobbed. "I don't know what happened. Please don't tell Daddy or your Granny. I'll be just fine."

"I won't," I promised, once again.

When we got home, Daddy was not there. The house stunk of whiskey and body odor. Mama quickly opened the windows and doors to air out the stench. Her movements were slow; she seemed so tired.

While Mama laid down on the ugly, gray couch, I turned on the television, and sat in Daddy's chair with the flattened seat cushion. A gentle breeze fluttered the curtains. "Mama, are you going to be all right?" I asked, afraid of her answer.

"Of course, I'm fine. I just need to rest. I'm going to close my eyes for a few minutes. You wake me up after Huntley-Brinkley is over. If you see Daddy coming, you wake me up right then," Mama said in a weak voice.

I sat staring at the television, glancing over at my mother, watching her chest raise and lower, making sure she was still alive.

CHAPTER TWO

Daddy came home early; I woke Mama as soon as I heard him stepping onto the porch. It was after eight, dusky dark. While Mama fixed him a skillet of chicken fried rice with scrambled eggs, I sat at my desk in my room, writing in my diary. Mama's younger sister, Aunt Betty, sent me a diary for my birthday, complete with a tiny lock and key. Often, I wrote page after page, about my normal things, the only things I knew, violence and fear. I hid the locked diary between my mattresses, and kept the key in my middle desk drawer.

"Susan, come in here and give me a big hug!" Daddy shouted from the kitchen.

I obeyed, wanting to keep peace. I entered the kitchen with outstretched arms, giving my father a warm generous hug. I hated it. After I sat down at the table, Mama placed a heaping dish of food in front of him, along with a tall glass of milk. He ate heartily.

"Sit down here," Daddy commanded to my mother.

Mama didn't say a word; she obeyed. The three of us sat in silence as Daddy enjoyed his food. Then, for no reason at all, he picked up the half-finished plate of food, hurled it against the wall, shattering the plate, and scattering the rice along the wall and linoleum floor.

"I can't eat all of this!" Daddy roared. "You're wasting food!"

We didn't say a word. Mama got up, and began cleaning up the mess. Daddy pushed his chair away from the table. As

13

Mama knelt to swipe up the bits of food, Daddy used his foot to push Mama down flat in the floor. He laughed as he walked into the living room, and sat in his old chair. I helped Mama clean up the best I could. The rice left tiny grease spots on the wall.

Luckily, Daddy fell asleep in his chair. We tiptoed around him, enjoying the reprieve. Yet, dread crept around with us. For reasons only known to God, Daddy woke up about eleven o'clock, and went to bed. Mama had laid down with me in my twin bed and fallen asleep. I could not bear to wake her, so I crawled out of bed, turned all the lights out, and checked the doors. As I returned to bed, I stumped my little toe on my chair, giving a muffled yelp. Unfortunately, that was enough to wake my mother. I whispered to her that Daddy was passed out in their bed. The moonlight shining through my bedroom window caught her smile. She hugged me before leaving my bed, telling me she wanted to sleep on the couch.

Tuesday was identical to the other weekdays, with one exception. Since the barbershop closed on Wednesdays, Daddy and his fishing buddy left for Norris Lake after work. Mama and I would be alone all Tuesday night. I always looked forward to Tuesday night, the one night I felt safe. Even Granny quipped that my lip wasn't dragging the ground.

At home that night, Mama and I ate hotdogs for supper, a treat for me. I noticed a bottle of pills on the kitchen counter. "What are those pills for? Are you sick?" I asked, holding the bottle up in an attempt to read the label.

"I went to the doctor today. After that fainting spell scared the daylights out of me in the car yesterday, I figured I'd better do something. Anyway, they checked my blood. The nurse told me she didn't see how in the world I was still walking around. The doctor said I had low blood. He gave me an iron shot, and these iron pills to build up my blood. He said it was the lowest he'd ever seen in a living body," Mama explained. "I wondered why I was so tired. He said that when I was better, I could just take Geritol instead of the pills."

Immediately, I became selfish in my thoughts. I panicked at the thought of my mother dying and leaving me with Daddy. "Oh, Mama, I'll help take care of you. Please don't get sick," I pleaded.

After supper, we sat out on the front porch, listening to the chatter of the crickets, and the croaking frogs. The end of August continued to supply the late evenings with a sticky, damp air. Neighbors across the street finished mowing their yard. Children played Steal the Bacon under the street lamp as the daylight faded. Lightning bugs scattered here and yon. Mama lit a cigarette, inhaling deep and long. I chose not to leave her sitting alone. I came to appreciate our time together, however brief it was.

"Susan, Labor Day is only a few days away. Everybody will be at Granny's for the holiday dinner," Mama said, while flicking cigarette ashes into the yard.

"Oh, I can't wait to see my cousins!" I said, pleased with the news. "Let's go up to Granny's early so we'll be there when they all come."

"Don't worry, we'll have to go early anyway because I have to help Granny cook," Mama said, as she got up out of the metal porch chair "Come on, Susan. It's time to go inside. The mosquitoes are eating me up."

After changing into our nightwear, we sat at the kitchen table, making a hillbilly milkshake. When we crumbled some cornbread in a tall glass, Mama poured milk in the glass up to the rim. We shared the treat, using two spoons. It was good to see Mama eat.

That night, we slumbered in our own beds. With the doors and windows left open to catch a breeze, the night sounds sang a lullaby. Deep in the mountains, a screech owl called a warning. Only twice did I jolt awake, breathless, unaccustomed to deep undisturbed sleep. Wednesday morning brought heavy sheets of

15

blowing rain. Mama ran into my room, and shut my window. I jumped up, helping her close the rest of the windows, fighting the pelting rain on my face. As we looked at each other, we laughed.

I thought of how much I loved my mother. "Mama, you look like an old wet dog," I giggled.

"You look like a drowned rat," she joked. "Go get a towel. Take off those wet pajamas, and put them in the bathtub. I'll hang them to dry later."

By the time I changed clothes, the rain had moved across the mountains. As I ate a bowl of cereal, Mama dressed for work. In the car, she turned on the radio, a rare treat, as she was always afraid of running down the battery. After we pulled up in front of Granny's house, I dared to ask, "Mama, when will Daddy be home?"

She pushed the hair out of my eyes. "He'll be home tonight . . . late, I guess. Try not to think about it," Mama replied, softly.

I helped Granny work in the garden that morning. The earlier rain had doused the naked tomato plants and empty green bean vines, creating a mess to be cleaned away. Nearly all the vegetables were canned or frozen, stashed in Granny's basement or in her freezer for the winter. Soon it would be time to tear down the corn stalks, and make ready the patch of ground for the winter. The soil on the banks of the Cumberland River proved to be fertile every year, even during times of drought. I liked digging in the dirt.

When Mama walked in Granny's house, I could tell there was something wrong. She practically scooted me out the door, hardly giving Granny time to talk to her at all. Once in the car, I asked her what was wrong. She told me that Daddy had called her, right before she got off work, to warn her that he was back. Mama's little body shook hard as she drove the old Ford.

Luckily, Daddy wasn't there when we got home. At least, we still had some time before he showed up. Usually he didn't come home until after dark. Mama cooked, rattling pots and pans, keeping her mind occupied with the present, not daring to think of what was to come. I ate quickly. Mama sat with me, drinking coffee, and chain-smoking. I tried to get her to eat, but she said she wasn't hungry.

The waiting was, sometimes, worse than the event. Yet, the anticipation paled in comparison to the nighttime terror. Later that night, as I laid in my bed, I heard a car door slam, then another. Wadding up the edge of my sheet, I squeezed it tight, just for something to hold onto. There was a knock on the door. Mama opened the door to a uniformed Kentucky State Policeman and Daddy. Outside, in front of our house, was a cruiser with another Trooper behind the wheel.

The policeman asked Mama if Daddy lived here, and she said "Yes." As the man turned to leave, Daddy thanked him for bringing him home, and stood at the door while the cruiser drove away. Then he came in, pushing Mama to the side, and slammed the door. Without a word, he went to bed. Mama told me later that Daddy had been drinking and playing cards at the American Legion. Two men at the card table accused Daddy of cheating. One pulled a knife on him. The bartender called the State Police to meet Daddy outside the building, and bring him home. I didn't know how Mama found out, whether Daddy told her or someone else, but Mama said it scared Daddy to death. "Too bad they didn't beat him up," I wrote in my diary.

Another night passed; we slept lightly. We left Daddy in the bed that morning. I was glad to leave. The house reeked of stale cigarettes and liquor sweat. No wonder Mama used so much Clorox. Once outside, the clean air put a smile on my face.

Mama's bald spots had scabbed over really good. Her purple marks faded into a shade of light green. Between getting some sleep and taking iron, she seemed to have more energy. I told her that she looked nice before she left me at Granny's. That seemed to please her.

For the next two days, Daddy behaved better than we ever expected. Mama said that he was still scared from that night at the American Legion. He came home two nights in a row right after work. He was almost pleasant as he sat in his chair with his half pint of Ancient Age whiskey. I didn't write in my diary those days because I felt like I would break the spell.

On Saturday, Daddy went fishing again, this time for the whole Labor Day weekend. Mama seemed so relieved because now she could spend more time up at Granny's with all the relatives without worrying about whether Daddy would make a scene. Instead of avoiding the truth as to why Daddy wasn't joining us, we could honestly say that he was at the lake.

Over the weekend, I heard no one ask where Daddy was, so I guess Mama told them up front that he went to the lake. My little cousin, Jane, and I played house with my dolls and had tea parties for everyone. My older cousin, Louise, and I played cowboys and Indians out in the yard. Being a teenager, she was forced to play with me. She took my cap pistol and rope, declaring herself the cowboy. That seemed fine . . . until she grabbed me, tied me to one of the mimosa trees, and left me there, crying. I screamed for help. Time passed slowly, although, it was only a few minutes. Granny looked out the kitchen window to see me tied to a tree. She came to my rescue, unwrapping the rope, and giving me a big hug. I told on Louise, but she didn't get punished.

On Labor Day, Mama, Granny, me, and all the aunts, uncles and cousins sat down to a huge dinner: fried chicken, corn-on-the-cob, mashed potatoes, green beans, yeast rolls, and cherry pie. There was so much food that our dinner plates heaped tall, nearly spilling over on the white linen tablecloth. Mama's iced tea never tasted better. By the time everyone had second helpings, the leftovers were sparse.

Those still sitting at the table after the pie and coffee reflected on the delicious fried chicken. Granny explained that it was better to fix a young chicken as the meat proved to be tender every time. She said that an old bird's body fried tough.

As I sat there, swallowing my last bite of pie, I couldn't remember seeing Blue in the back yard. I jumped up, ran to the back screen door, looking out, called my chicken by name. I ran back to the dining room, meeting the eyes of everyone at the table, including Granny's.

"Oh, Susan, I'm so sorry. I just didn't think," Granny pleaded, her face showing true remorse, and a little embarrassment.

"Granny! You killed Blue!" I cried. "And, I ate my chicken!"

Mama and her sisters turned their heads to keep from laughing. They knew I was heartbroken. My uncles were in the living room watching television, unconcerned about my devastating loss. Louise was no where to be found at the moment and Jane couldn't have cared less. Granny reached out her arms, and I fell into her embrace. I would write about this in my diary.

That afternoon, when all the relatives were gone, Mama vacuumed, dusted, and straightened Granny's house back to perfect order. All the dishes were back in the cabinets, the table linens removed, the chairs in place, and the stove and counter wiped clean. On the front porch, I sat in the glider with Granny. She mentioned how much she missed my Daddy not being there to share in the holiday. I didn't respond. I couldn't lie to my Granny . . . unless Mama said to.

Having three days of peace nearly spoiled us. Yet, as soon as we stepped into our home, a deep sadness immediately shrouded our faces. We waited for the unexpected; we didn't have to wait long. Daddy arrived in full force late that night.

He tiptoed into my room as I pretended to be asleep, taking my record player and Ray Charles 33⅓ records. In the kitchen, he sat at the table playing his records, and drinking out of a bottle of Early Times. The songs were wistful and deep, and I almost felt a twinge of pity. I heard Mama tell him that I needed some school clothes. Then the gates of hell opened. I got out of bed, stood at my doorway, peeping into the kitchen. Daddy jumped up, grabbing Mama by the arm, twisting it behind her back. She let out a garbled noise, trying not to wake me. She begged him to let go as he dragged her around in the kitchen, pushing her against the counter, then the stove. Ray Charles still played. Mama broke loose, and ran into the living room. He chased after her, grabbing her by the hair of her head, slinging her backwards onto the coffee table, breaking it. Mama let out a horrible moan. I couldn't stand it any longer. I ran to her, helping her up off the wooden table, and sitting her on the couch.

Standing there, Daddy finally spoke, "Hi, honey, did you have a good time up at your Granny's?"

I turned to look at this man that I hardly knew. "Yes, Daddy, I did," I answered.

"Well, that's good," he said as he ambled back to the kitchen where the needle was scratching the end of the record on the player.

He turned the player off and finished his bottle. Mama and I sat together on the couch. I rubbed her arm. I wanted to get some ice to put on it but didn't want to go in the kitchen. After Daddy went to bed, Mama and I slept together in my twin bed. I told her I was afraid to sleep by myself that night, but the truth was that I didn't want her to be alone.

The next morning, while I was getting dressed, Mama made my bed. Usually I made my own bed, but, this time, she decided to make it since we were running a little late. Unfortunately, I left the key in the diary lock. She opened it, reading far too much. Not knowing what else to write about, I wrote about life with Daddy. Through the misspelled scribble, she read details of my nights, and some of my days. She brought the book to me as I was brushing my teeth.

"Susan, honey, you can't write about this. What if somebody found it, and read it? I'm sorry," Mama said, handing me the diary. "Put it in the garbage after you tear up the pages."

I rinsed my toothbrush, spit, and looked up at her hurtful expression. I felt angry that she had read my most private thoughts; I knew my writing hurt her. "Okay, Mama, I'm sorry," I said, suddenly regretting that I ever wrote a word in that book.

After filling the garbage pail with ripped paper, I folded the brown paper sack, and took it outside to the big metal can. In the meantime, Mama waited for me at the back door. Before we left, we looked in on Daddy, the covers pulled up around his head. I wondered if he was dead. I closed the door behind me.

My father cut hair at the local barber shop in town. Because he had a gift of making people laugh, he kept a large list of customers. I never knew that side of him.

Before Mama stopped at Granny's, she reminded me that school started the next day. "I am going to get you some school clothes at Powers & Hortons today. I may run in Bowers for a pair of shoes. You really don't need very much until it gets cold weather. That is, unless you take a growing spurt," Mama said, trying to ease me into the new school year.

I kept thinking of how she was going to pay for it. "That's okay. Don't worry. I can still wear my old clothes. I don't need anything," I assured her. "It doesn't matter, really."

"Look, you will have new clothes for school. I will charge it, if I have to. I've got a good standing account at those stores, and they know I will pay," Mama said, a tear falling down her cheek. "I always pay my bills."

I had a hard time being nice to Granny that day, still in mourning over my chicken. I kept quiet until noon. Then, deciding that was long enough to punish my grandmother, I silently forgave her as we ate our boloney sandwiches. I don't think she noticed.

CHAPTER THREE

My first day back to Holy Trinity Catholic School was better than I expected. Two rooms in the basement of the Catholic church provided eight grades, first through fourth on one side, and fifth through eight on the other side. Two Sisters of Notre Dame taught four grades each. My teacher looked like the statue of the Virgin Mary in church, her brown eyes soulful, her skin fair and delicate. She had been my teacher last school year. I liked her a lot.

The other teacher nun, who taught the upper grades, was old, about fifty, and waddled when she walked. She kept her hand on her rosary beads all the time, praying, I guess. I got the idea that she didn't like children. One day the year before, as I was within an earshot, I overheard her mumble a bad word. It embarrassed me even though no one else heard it. I never told anyone about it.

Mama and I went to school early that morning so I could get my books, find my assigned seat, and meet any new students. Dottie and her sister were there with their mother. I had only seen Dottie a few times and at church during the summer, so the reunion was more than special. After Mama talked with my teacher, she left for work. I didn't mind. I was in the fourth grade.

The first week went by quickly. Homework consisted of short repetitious lessons of the last school year. I figured the teacher thought some of her students may have forgotten their learning.

I did the assignments simply because I enjoyed it. I loved the smell of blackboard chalk, new writing paper, and number two sharpened pencils. I considered becoming a teacher.

Mama's birthday came and went. Granny gave her ten dollars in a nice Hallmark card. She got birthday cards from her two sisters and brother. All I had to give was a big hug and kiss. She was thirty-six. Daddy didn't even wish her "Happy Birthday."

By the end of third week, I had adjusted to school life. Dottie's mother always picked us up after school. Usually, she dropped me off at Granny's since Mama was still working. I didn't mind because I could do my homework before I got home . . . and before Daddy showed up.

On Friday, Dottie asked me to spend the night with her. I was elated, for I had never spent the night in someone else's home other than my Granny's. Reluctant at first to let me go, Dottie's mother assured my mother that we would be fine. So, after packing a little bag, Mama drove me to Dottie's house about six in the evening, just in time for supper. I became embarrassed with all Mama's kisses and hugs. When she finally did drive away, I felt a pang if guilt. I would not be there to protect her when Daddy came home.

At Dottie's house, everyone sat at the table for supper. Her father talked, asking me questions about school, talking about a new television show called *Father Knows Best*, laughing with his daughters. I felt confused. I answered politely, focused on my plate of food, and used my best manners. Dottie and her sister argued playfully, their mother ignoring their antics. After supper, Dottie and I washed the dishes while her parents sat in the small living room talking in pleasant, low tones. By comparison my home life was a nightmare. I hardly slept because of this revelation. I became consumed with envy.

The following morning, Dottie's mother came into the bedroom, pulled the curtains back on the window, and raised the shades to bright streams of sunshine. She sang a sweet melody as she shook the end of our twin bed. The aroma of fried sausage, scrambled eggs, and homemade biscuits, enticed me to quickly get dressed and sit at their kitchen table. The house felt calm, cheerful. I wondered if I had stepped into a world like *Father Knows Best* because, as far as I knew, this life just did not exist.

Mama came to get me around about one o'clock. Dottie's mother told her we behaved well, and that I was welcome to come back soon. That pleased me. Even with Dottie's pesky sister, I enjoyed every minute of my stay.

As soon as I saw Mama, I noticed her swollen bottom lip. Sitting in the front seat on the way home, I asked her if she had a cold sore on her mouth.

"No, honey, that was your Daddy last night. He kept me up all night long, well, til four this morning. He chased me outside, and locked the door for a couple of hours, maybe longer, I just don't know. Then, when he unlocked the door, I waited a few minutes, thinking he might come after me in the dark, and I'd have a chance to run," Mama rambled. "But, when I thought he'd gone to bed, I sneaked inside. He was waiting; that's when he slapped me. I just got through cleaning the blood off the rug before I came to pick you up."

Now, I felt so guilty. *I shouldn't have left her. Maybe I'm not supposed to have a nice time*, I thought. "Mama, I'm sorry. Please don't be mad at me," I begged.

"I'm not mad at you. It wasn't your fault, it's your Daddy," Mama replied. "I'm glad you went to Dottie's."

The rest of the day, my thoughts bounced from Dottie's house to my house, the similarities and the differences. I concluded there was nothing similar between our families. If Dottie's home was normal, then, what was mine? I needed to find out.

Daddy left before we arrived back home. Mama said that he went fishing and wouldn't return until Sunday evening. A relief washed over me. I needed some quiet time to sort things out. Mama needed time to heal . . . again.

"Susan, get in the closet, and get the basket of dirty clothes. I'm going to wash a load of whites today. The sun is shining warm, even though the air is a little cool. They'll dry in no time," Mama said, as she got the bottle of Clorox and Tide detergent out from under the sink.

As I gathered some spilled clothes on the closet floor, I noticed the lid on the shoe box with the gun inside was slightly open. When I looked closer, I saw the broken kite string. I raised the lid; the gun was gone; the bullets were still there. I didn't know who took the gun, and I figured I shouldn't ask any questions.

Trying to make up for what Daddy did to her the night before, without me there to protect her, I stayed close to my mother the rest of the day. On the wall, next to the front door, I found some tiny blood spots. Trying to remove the specks, I rubbed them into the paint, only making it more noticeable. I didn't tell Mama.

Because I didn't sleep well at Dottie's, I fell quickly into a deep sleep that night in my own bed. I woke up on Sunday morning with my rosary beads still under my pillow. I had planned on saying a rosary before going to sleep, asking for help, but I didn't get past the first "Hail Mary."

Mama had built a fire in the coal furnace during the night to keep the cold air from creeping through the cracks in the walls. The autumn sun gave false hope of its warmth. A light frost glistened on the oaks, maples, and poplars, giving the leaves a beginning of deep crimson, tangy orange, and lemon yellow. The cloudless sky spanned a blanket of bright blue from mountain top to mountain top. Mama and I enjoyed the drive to church that morning.

After services, we stopped by Granny's house to see if she wanted to go home with us for a while. Instead, she offered us homemade soup and fresh lemon pie. We stayed there until late afternoon, not planning to, but Mama didn't seem in a big hurry to get home.

25

Because the harsh winters kept Granny indoors, she stayed busy by quilting. So after dinner, Mama helped Granny get her bag of quilting pieces out of the closet, oiled the Singer, and counted the spools of thread. They sat at the kitchen table reviewing patterns of The Dutch Girl, Windmill, and Wedding Ring. Granny usually made two quilts each winter, depending on who was getting married, or who was having a baby in the family. Sometimes, she just gave a quilt away to a family friend. Mama had three quilts already: one for marrying, one for having me, and one just because.

By five o'clock, the sun played peek-a-boo on the mountain ridges and we were back home. Sadly, the house was cold; the fire had gone out since no one was home to feed the furnace. After adding a bucket of coal and rekindling the fire, Mama brought the warmth back into the house.

Mama took a bath first. She stood in front of the mirror when I opened the bathroom door, thinking she had already dressed. Her body wrapped in a bath towel, it could not hide the black and blue marks on her back. I tried not to stare; yet, I wondered if those bruises were old or fresh.

Knowing that the next day was a school day, I laid my clothes out, collected my textbooks, and was in bed early. I figured that I needed to try to get some sleep before Daddy came home. I told Mama to go to bed too, but she just sat in the living room, her hand trembling with a lit cigarette between her fingers.

My little alarm clock showed one a.m. when my Daddy burst through the door. With no attempt to be quiet, he stomped through the house, not stopping at my door this time. His voice turned to raging screams as he commanded Mama to come in the kitchen. She obeyed. I heard her ask if he had eaten, and he yelled something about her never cooking a meal for him. Then I heard the clanging of pots and pans, so I assumed she was fixing him a meal. Hearing shuffling feet, I got up out of bed and crouched down beside my doorway to see what was going on.

Daddy pulled Mama away from the stove, and pushed her down in a kitchen chair. He stood over top of her, his tongue thick, his voice incoherent. I felt real fear; this time was different. He pulled a gun out of his pocket.

"What are you doing, Quinton?" Mama hollered, trying to get up from the chair. "Where did you get that gun?"

Daddy pushed Mama back down in the chair with his free hand. "I thought we could play a little game tonight, just you and me," he threatened, as he put the 38 Smith & Wesson to her head and cocked the hammer. "Maybe Russian Roulette?"

"Oh, please put it away. Oh, God!" Mama cried, putting her hands over her face.

I didn't know what to do. I froze, part of me wanting to run in there and the other part wanting to run away.

Daddy roared with laughter. "Hell, Jewell, it ain't loaded. See?" he said, as he raised the gun toward the ceiling and pulled the trigger. The shot went through the ceiling making a perfect round hole. Daddy jumped, Mama screamed, and I broke loose from my trance. I ran in the kitchen to see my father in a stupor, not really aware that I was standing there. I grabbed Mama's arm and pulled her into the living room. We went out the front door and sat in the car for a long time. It was cold, and we were barefooted. We had no place to go, and even if we did, we didn't have the car keys. So we sneaked into the yard, and peeked into the bedroom window, seeing Daddy laying in bed. Fortunately, the door was unlocked so we sneaked back inside the warm house. Mama slept with me that night.

In the morning, Mama found the gun on the kitchen counter. She hid it in an opening in the ceiling inside the food pantry. Daddy would never find it there. Then before we left the house, Mama slipped into the bedroom and raised the window, allowing the early cold air to circle the bed where her husband slept. She shut the bedroom door.

"Mama, why'd you do that?" I whispered, as we got in the car.

"I don't know. Maybe, he'll freeze to death," she replied, crisply. "Don't tell anybody about last night, please. Do it for me."

"Okay," I said, not really knowing what my response should have been.

At school, I busied myself in listening intently to the teacher, completing my assignments, just being happy to be away from home. It didn't last. At lunch time, as everyone ate their sack lunches, Daddy came into the room. Looking handsome in his light weight brown coat, his black hair meticulously combed, and a wide grin on his face, he spoke with my teacher for a few minutes before coming over to my desk. I hoped I was dreaming a nightmare.

"Hello, sweetheart. I've got a surprise for you," he said, bending down to kiss my cheek.

Smelling his breath nearly made me puke. I looked up at him, and smiled, terrified as to whatever was going to happen.

"Children, Susan's father has brought us all a wonderful surprise. Each one of you will get an ice cream treat after you eat your lunch. That is very generous of Mr. Noe, so you must thank him before he leaves," the teacher announced.

"Thank you, Mr. Noe!" the whole classroom of children chimed.

I just sat there. Did he really think he could make up to me about last night? He acted as if we were the happiest father and daughter in Harlan County. Was I supposed to forgive him like the Bible says, and just go on like nothing ever happened? Or was this a bribe to keep my mouth shut? He needn't have worried; Mama already made me promise.

After he left, the teacher gave out the little cups of vanilla ice cream with small wooden spoons. I endured the rest of the afternoon, listening to praises for my Daddy from the teacher and other students. My stomach felt like a bag of jumping beans. I got the hiccups in the middle of the history lesson, and had to excuse myself for a drink of water.

For the next two weeks, Daddy came home soon after work. Never on time for supper, he ate alone at the kitchen table. In the evenings, he sat in the living room, watching television. Mama stayed in the kitchen. I don't think she could bear to look at him. Although Mama and I didn't talk about it, we feared his act would come to an end. An occasional raised voice felt tolerable compared to Daddy's usual behavior. He caught himself several times starting to escalate and quickly lowered his loud dictatorial tone. He drank straight from the bottle of Kentucky bourbon, not even making a screwed-up face as the liquid burned down his throat. He smacked his lips. I sat on the couch across from Daddy, staring at the television. Every time he would holler at Mama, my insides jumped. She told me later that shooting that gun must have scared the daylights out of him, so, just maybe, he was trying to change. I knew better than that.

On Sunday, Daddy drove Granny back down to our house for dinner. He was attentive, polite, not the man who lived in my home. Baffled, it was difficult for me to know what was real. Had I imagined all those sleepless nights? Was something wrong with me? Was I crazy?

At the dinner table, I decided to go for broke, asking if Dottie could spend the night on Friday. As Granny looked on, Daddy agreed. I was "Daddy's little girl." Mama nearly choked on her bite of meatloaf. I knew I was taking a huge risk, having my best friend spend all night. If Daddy ranted like a lunatic, Dottie would never speak to me again. If Daddy behaved himself, then, I would have found a way to get a night's sleep. I was willing to take that chance.

My father was a great actor with good looks and great charm. He joined the Little Harlan Theater Group earlier that year, and on Monday, February 10, 1958, Daddy took on the role of Lawrence Regan, a New York gangster in *The Night of January 16th*. He wowed the audience with his portrayal of an underworld thug. Little did they know how closely his acting resembled real life.

29

The week passed quickly; partly because Daddy remained somewhat civil. I was beginning to have a little hope. On Friday, Dottie's mother let me and Dottie off at Mama's office after school. We had about an hour and a half before Mama got off of work so we went to Creech Drug Store, and drank a fountain coke at the counter. Then we walked to the barber shop to see Daddy: I wanted to remind him that Dottie was spending the night, just in case.

Although busy wrapping a hot towel over a customer's face, Daddy acknowledged us with a wink when he saw us peeking inside the shop. "Hello, girls. How about a haircut?" Daddy joked.

"I don't think so. I just wanted to let you know that Dottie's spending the night tonight," I said, hoping he would get the hint.

He took the hot towel off the man's face, stirred the soapy shaving mug, and began to lather the man's beard. He turned, looking directly at me. "That's fine, Susan. I'll see if I can make it home a little early tonight."

We said our good-byes, and returned to Mama's office just in time for her to leave. We stopped at Granny's house for only a few minutes, just to see if she was okay, and then we went home. While Dottie and I wrapped up in a blanket on the couch, Mama built a fire in the furnace. It didn't take long for the heat to start rushing through the floor registers.

Soon, the smell of catfish frying in the cast iron skillet tantalized our hungry stomachs. As the three of us sat down to our meatless Friday supper, Mama asked Dottie to say the blessing. Before I put the first bite of macaroni and cheese in my mouth, the man I called Daddy came through the front door, with a smile on his face. Supper was like no other that I ever remembered. Both my parents made a considerable effort to mimic a "happy family," and I was nearly speechless.

After the dishes were washed and put up, Dottie and I played records in my room until time to go to bed. I heard mumbling from the kitchen, but nothing to anticipate embarrassment. Later, as my friend and I crawled into my bed, Daddy came into my room with a flashlight. He turned off my lamp. I was stunned. Dottie giggled.

Daddy turned on the flashlight, turning the beam up under his chin, making him look like a monster. "I am here to tell you a scary story. That is, if you're not afraid," he growled.

Dottie and I laughed. "We're not afraid!" we chimed.

Daddy sat on the edge of the bed, and told a ghost story about a young girl who died mysteriously on top of Booger Mountain. It seemed that the ghost could be seen in the back seat of a car when someone traveled at night over the mountain. By the time Daddy was finished, Dottie and I had the covers nearly over our heads. I saw a wonderful side of my father that I never knew existed. How I wished the moment was frozen in time so that I might visit it again.

On Saturday morning, Daddy was already gone by the time Dottie and I woke up. I wondered if it had all been a dream. We ate cinnamon rolls for breakfast while Mama started polishing the living room furniture and vacuuming. Before lunch, Dottie's mother came to pick her up; I hated to see her leave. For that one night, I had a family, a fake one, but that was fine with me.

CHAPTER FOUR

Nothing lasts forever, good or bad. That Friday night proved to be the last of the "Happy Family on Bailey Street." For the next few weeks, Daddy reverted to the raving, violent drunk that I knew best. It wasn't hard for me to adjust to: no sleep, upset stomach, trembling hands, and shallow breathing. As Halloween approached, I tried to look forward to trick or treating. Daddy cut out a jack-o-lantern from a pumpkin. As he wielded the butcher knife, carving out the eyes, nose, and mouth, I became somewhat uneasy. It was as if he was enjoying it a little too much, with every gouge. Together, we set the jack-o-lantern on the front porch. He scared me more when he was nice.

Halloween brought the usual ghosts and goblins to our door. A cold drizzle all that day caused a heavy fog to loom from mountain tops draping over the hollers. Sinister barren trees created a haunting scene as the street lights threw shadows as darkness fell. Daddy was not home when I left the house with my little paper sack. Mama sat on the porch, giving out candy. Deciding I was too old for a costume, I walked along the sidewalks trying to mingle with kids going door-to-door. Turning the corner, I saw some boys throwing eggs on the side of a house. The slick wet leaves sticking to my shoes made it impossible for me to run away so I squatted down near a hedge until they left. It didn't take long for me to fill my sack with candy, wax whistles, popcorn balls, and candy apples. The damp night air clung to my clothes; mists of white breath puffed from my mouth. The cold seeped into my body just as a sudden downpour drenched the little town, causing the trick or treaters to scatter. I stayed out as long as I could, dreading the evil inside my house as much as fearing the monsters roaming the streets on Halloween. I walked slowly through the rain, preparing myself for the unknown. Just maybe he won't come home, maybe he will disappear into the wet blackness of night and no one will ever find him, or maybe he went to bed. That was a fleeting thought as it was only nine p.m. and I figured that he wouldn't come home til after midnight. At least, that was his usual pattern . . . but not this time.

As I neared my house, I noticed the porch light was off. At first, I decided that the rain had driven Mama inside but when I stepped upon the porch, I could hear my father's roars. I turned the doorknob but it was locked. I heard the desperate pleading voice of Mama. I knocked, then banged on the door. Silence. No one came. I beat on the window pane and then again on the door.

As I turned to run across the street to a neighbor's house, Mama opened the door. Her dark matted hair around her tear-stained face told me it was bad. "Hurry up, Susan, get in here," she whispered. "He's in the bathroom."

"Are you all right?" I asked while looking passed her into the living room and the kitchen. I handed her my bag of goodies. Suddenly, the treats were unimportant.

"You're soaking wet. Go take those clothes off and I'll bring you a towel. Don't turn on your light, just get your pajamas on and get in bed. Maybe he won't notice," Mama said as she rushed me into my bedroom.

I grabbed the towel from Mama as she tossed it to me in the dimly lit room. The street light shining through my window gave me just enough light to change clothes. I pulled the covers over my head and clasped my hands in prayer. My hair, still damp, gave a musty odor underneath the sheets.

Feeling the urge to cough, I smothered the noise against my pillow. It wasn't enough. Hearing Daddy stomp through the house, I held my breath. He staggered into my bedroom and flipped the light switch on. Even under the covers, I smelled him.

"Susan, when did you get home?" he demanded, jerking my bedcovers down to my knees.

"Daddy, I went trick or treating. This is Halloween," I answered, pulling the sheet back on me.

"Don't you talk back to me, little girl! Seems you're getting too big for your britches. Your mother lets you do whatever you want and that is going to stop!" Daddy rambled.

With quiet steps, Mama hurried to rescue her daughter. I don't know if Daddy knew that Mama was standing behind him when he reeled around with a raised fist, hitting Mama in the head. Her body flew like a bird until she fell onto the coffee table. The force broke a table leg for the second time but Mama looked like a broken doll.

I jumped out of bed, pushed past Daddy who stood there speechless, and cradled Mama in my arms. "Mama!"

Daddy mumbled something and went back in the kitchen, leaving me and Mama in the living room floor.

"Go back to bed, honey," Mama said as I helped her stand up. "I'm all right."

"But, Mama . . . " I started.

In a raging furor, Daddy returned to the living room wielding a butcher knife, drooling as he spouted incoherently. He grabbed Mama by her hair and dragged her into their bedroom. I followed, pulling on his arm trying to make him release her. While Mama wailed, I screamed, and Daddy bellowed. He threw Mama on the full size bed.

"I'm tired of not knowing where you are either. So you get in this bed too," Daddy yelled while pointing the knife at my face. His face distorted, his eyes glared wildly.

I obeyed, not saying a word for fear it would make things worse. So that night, Daddy passed out on one side of the bed still holding the butcher knife. Mama laid motionless in the middle while I stayed awake on the other side, just in case. Laying there, I stared out the window watching a beautiful moon come out of hiding as the clouds parted. I begged God to help us and closed my eyes.

As the morning broke daylight, I awoke to hear Daddy snoring loudly. The room reeked of all the familiar odors. I found Mama sitting at the kitchen table drinking her coffee, already dressed for work. She looked so pretty in her navy shirtwaist dress. The long sleeves covered her bruises nicely. Her hair shaped differently around her face but I figured it was to hide her bald spots. She wore pearl clip-on earrings, a present last Christmas from her sister in Somerset.

Mama acted as if it was just another day. "Good morning, Susan, I was getting ready to wake you. Hurry and get dressed. Granny is waiting on us. You know she can't go to the barn until I drop you off."

Because Mama now had to work half a day on Saturdays, I had no choice but to stay at Granny's. I didn't mind.

For a brief minute, I sat at the table with my mother, watching her, thinking of how could she do this? How could she pretend that everything was fine? I was afraid to ask.

After dressing in my brown corduroy pants and flannel shirt, I quickly ate a bowl of cereal. I didn't like cereal, but that was the only way to get the toy prize hidden down in the bottom of the box. Eating one bowl a day created an eternity until the box emptied.

As Mama waited at the front door, I grabbed my jacket and we left, leaving our troubles inside the walls of the tiny house. *Maybe it will catch on fire,* I thought.

Taking less than ten minutes to get to Granny's house, there wasn't much time for conversation. But then Mama and I never really talked about much of anything. She seemed so far away most of the time, lost in her own world, a world I wasn't a part of. Before I got out of the car in front of Granny's house, I mustered up enough courage and asked, "Mama, why don't we run away?"

Visibly irritated by my question, Mama's smile turned stiff. "Susan, quit being ridiculous. There's no place to go. Now you be a good girl for me and I'll pick you up after work. Tell Granny the reason I didn't come in is because I'm running late for work. Go on, now."

I stood on Granny's front porch and watched my mother's car disappear around the curve. I waved but I knew she didn't see me. That was okay.

The hours went by quickly, especially since the Saturday morning cartoons consumed the three television stations. I didn't mind that Granny spent a lot of time at the barn or in the yard. She worked hard every day, never one to just sit. I enjoyed being by myself. Her home always smelled of furniture polish and fresh air.

About one o'clock, Mama came, carrying a sack of groceries. She placed the sack on the kitchen table. "Mother, I stopped at the A&P and picked up a few things. You can pay me later," Mama said.

"Now I wish you hadn't done that. I've got plenty," Granny fussed. "It doesn't take much to feed me and I've got a freezer full of garden stuff."

"Well, I know that. Let's just say that I got it for when Susan stays here," Mama suggested.

I peeked inside the sack and spied a can of lima beans. "Mama, you know I don't like lima beans!"

"Susan, hush!" Mama barked, lightly smacking my hand away from the sack. "Are you ready to go?"

"Do you want to take some of this home?" Granny asked, peeking inside the sack.

"For heaven sakes, let me just leave it here and if I need anything, I will get it," Mama pleaded.

My grandmother was never one to just accept a gift of any kind whether she needed it or not. It seemed she was bound to argue or try to give it back. Before Granddaddy, a coal miner, had died the year before from Black Lung, it had been a difficult time because he had been sick for so long. She sold eggs, chickens, and garden produce to pay the bills. She was too proud to ask for help from anyone. After his death, Granny was too young to get social security so things changed from bad to worse. Granny had no choice but to accept help from her children. Her son, working at the Miner's Hospital, helped out along with her three daughters. Mama found it easier to buy groceries rather than try to give her money. It avoided embarrassment between the two of them.

During our ride home, I wondered if Daddy was still in the bed. I know Mama was thinking the same thing because when she parked the car in front of the house, I watched her face turn pale as if her blood drained right before my eyes. I took a deep breath as we walked upon the porch. I wanted to fly away, far away, like Peter Pan . . . and Mama could be Wendy . . . and we'd live happily ever after, just me and Mama.

Once inside the house, I was thankful to discover Daddy wasn't there, and neither was his fishing gear. It was as if the rooms changed from gloom to brightness, knowing that he was at the lake and we would get to sleep that night. I tried to help Mama clean house but she always went behind me, cleaning it for a second time. Then she finished her ironing. Sprinkling the clothes from a water-filled RC bottle plugged with a holey stopper, she ironed everything, including the sheets, towels, and underwear. I was not allowed to touch the iron so I watched television thinking if I didn't aggravate her, she would get done quicker. It worked. We ate soup and grilled cheese sandwiches for supper, one of my favorite meals. Before dark, Mama carried a bucket of coal inside the furnace room and stoked the fire. Taking advantage of the warm house, I eagerly took a bath in the claw tub. I used little hot water, saving some for Mama. After I dressed for bed, it was Mama's turn to bathe. It took longer than usual so I knocked on the bathroom door. I felt I had to protect her from the unseen and unexpected since I wasn't doing such a good job keeping her safe from Daddy.

"Are you all right, Mama?" I hollered.

"I'm just fine, honey," she answered. "I'll be out in a minute."

Mama fixed popcorn and we sat on the old gray couch. She thumbed through a magazine while I watched television. It was comfortable. By nine p.m., we were in our beds. It was glorious and I thanked God over and over until I drifted off to sleep.

Sunday morning came too quickly. We dressed for church, barely making it in time for Confession before Mass. As I knelt in the confessional, looking through the screen to the priest on the other side and asking him to bless me for I had sinned, I wanted so badly to ask him to help Mama. But the words failed to come out of my mouth. Instead, I told him that I had kept bad thoughts that week, not telling him the thoughts involved wanting the house to catch on fire with Daddy in it. I received absolution along with penance of several Hail Mary's and Our Father's. I felt cleansed and took Communion with a pure heart. I knew it was wrong to want bad things to happen to Daddy but I didn't know how to stop it. So I prayed for God to stop it before Daddy killed my mother. It was just that simple.

After Mass, Dottie and I talked outside on the church steps while Mama lit a candle and prayed. Dottie hinted for me to ask her to come home with me but I was afraid Daddy would come home early. After a few minutes, I saw Mama walking toward us, giving me an excuse to get inside the car. I felt that Dottie got mad at me but I couldn't take the chance. I would see her in school the next day anyway and try to make it up to her.

Mama and I stopped at Granny's on the way home. The wonderful aroma of fried pork chops and fresh baked cornbread enticed us to stay for Sunday dinner. Mama explained that Daddy went fishing. Nothing else was mentioned about it. After the dinner, we all went to Resthaven Cemetery to visit Grand-daddy. Almost every Sunday, we paid our respects at his grave. Although they wept openly, I never cried. I loved my grandfather but I just didn't feel sad, not like them.

Before driving Granny back home, we stopped at Mike's Drive-In. I enjoyed sitting in between Mama and Granny in the front seat of the car. The heater blew warmth on our feet and legs. We were the three musketeers, with ice cream cones.

As we dropped Granny off at her house, the sense of dread moved into my thoughts. Now we had to go home . . . and I didn't know what or who was waiting. I often wondered if Granny knew there was something wrong in our house, that an evil in a whiskey bottle ruled our lives. She never said a word.

I spent the rest of the afternoon sitting at the kitchen table, doing my homework while Mama polished a pair of her high heels, hemmed a pair of slacks, and wrote checks to pay the bills. It seemed that we were getting prepared. The weekend was over and we knew it. A depression covered us like a heavy quilt.

For whatever reason, we never found out why Daddy came home after midnight and went straight to bed. Mama slept with me that night. We heard him come in, mumbling and stumbling, but then quiet. I started to whisper but she put her hand over my mouth. The seconds ticked, then minutes passed. Hallelujah! We heard snoring! What a wonderful surprise! We closed our eyes.

The next day, after a quick breakfast of cereal and toast, I dressed for school. After collecting my books and lunch-box, we left Daddy in the bed and went on with our lives. The crisp cold air felt so good, like being renewed, or rising from the dead. Mama drove to Rio Vista to pick up Dottie and her little sister. The conversation was light and funny, almost as if last night never happened. After Mama dropped us off at school, she went to work.

At my desk, I found it hard to concentrate, the words on the pages of my history book blurred, running together at times. *If I could just rest*, I thought, my eyes rolling back in my head, fighting the urge to lay my head do and pretend to be sick. Mama continually insisted I strive for perfection, no excuses. The teachers expected no less either. Yet, I didn't feel that I was smart enough for the teachers or important enough to have friends, other than Dottie, of course. In fact, she was my only friend. I didn't feel good enough about myself to join in school activities. I was a follower, not a leader. The only thing I knew about was survival.

The following week brought a surprise snow, nearly four inches deep. School was called off which meant I got to stay at Granny's house. Being a very careful driver, Mama took her time driving through the snow on the narrow two lane road to Granny's house and on to work.

Between Daddy's rants and lack of sleep, I welcomed the time I could snuggle upon Granny's couch with one of her handmade quilts and a soft pillow. While she sewed on her Dutch Girl quilt, I watched television, sleeping most of the afternoon. By the time Mama picked me up from work, it looked like most of the snow had melted.

When Mama opened Granny's back door, a blast of cold air preceded her. She didn't even take her coat off.

"Mother, the roads are freezing back over. It's going to be bad tonight. I don't know if there will be school tomorrow but I'll call you as soon as I hear," Mama puffed. "Come on, Susan, we have to get home. The fire is probably out, I'll need to build one before it gets dark."

"Bring the child back up here in the morning if you need to. I don't mind the company," Granny said.

The ride back home was in dead silence as Mama gripped the steering wheel, not taking her eyes off the road as we went around the curves. On my right was the ice-covered Cumberland

River. On the left side, the trees, heavy with freezing drizzle, hung over the road. If it had not been so scary, it would have been a white wonderland.

Sure enough, the fire was out in the furnace. The house was bitter cold. Mama filled the coffee pot and changed into her old clothes. Keeping my coat on, I wrapped up in a blanket on the couch while Mama went to the furnace room to fill the coal bucket with cinders out of the furnace. I heard her carry the bucket outside to empty it in a barrel. As she opened the back door bringing in a bucket of coal for the fire, I heard her scream. I threw the blanket off of me and ran to the back door leading into the furnace room. I saw Mama bending over hopping on one foot, with one hand on the door knob and the other hand still holding the bucket of coal.

"Mama, what's wrong?" I hollered.

"I stepped on something. Come and help me in!" she cried.

I took the bucket of coal, pulling and scooting it to the furnace, too heavy for me to lift. I helped her start a fire with the block coal and a few pieces of kindling. Then she hobbled into the kitchen and sat down. She was so cold. Luckily, the heat registers were blowing warm air quickly and soon the house began to thaw.

She pulled her right foot upon her left knee to look at the bottom of her shoe. It was wet, sooty from the coal, and bloody. She ran her hand over the sole. "Oh, Susan, I've got a nail in my foot. Ohhhhh, it hurts so bad," she sobbed. "Go in the bathroom, get me a wet washrag and the merthiolate. Get a strip of cloth out the small sack underneath the sink."

By the time I brought the things back to her, she had already pulled the nail out of her foot and taken her shoe off. With tears streaming down her face, she wiped the blood and dirt off of her foot. I watched her put the merthiolate around the hole in the bottom of her heel. She cried out as she wrapped it with a thin strip of an old sheet and slipped a sock over the foot.

Now I understood why Mama never threw anything away, even thread-worn sheets.

"Mama, let me help you to the couch and you can put your foot up," I suggested. "Do you want me to call the doctor?"

"No, don't call the doctor. If it's no better by tomorrow, I'll go by his office at lunch time," she said. "No need for him to come down here in this weather."

I helped her to the couch and laid the blanket over her. I could almost see her heart beating fiercely in her little chest. I set a cup of coffee and her cigarettes on the end table next to her. Then I fixed us each a baloney sandwich for supper, not knowing how to cook. Mama only took a bite or two, but I refilled her cup twice.

Watching Mama's eyes close, I tried to be quiet so to give her some peaceful sleep. For the next few hours, I kept vigil on my mother, sometimes standing over her. She looked so old and she was only thirty-six. I was afraid to leave her for my bed so I sat in Daddy's ugly old chair. Finally, I laid my head on the armrest and fell asleep.

Startled by the front door slamming against the wall as Daddy walked in, I jerked and hollered, waking Mama.

"What in the hell, is going on here?" Daddy yelled, standing in the living room with his hands on his hips in defiance. "Why aren't you in bed, Susan?"

"Daddy, Mama stepped on a nail getting the coal in," I answered. "The fire was out."

"Go to bed. Now!" Daddy insisted, pointing his finger to my bedroom. "I'll take care of this."

Mama looked at me and nodded. I didn't want to leave her but if I didn't do what he said, it might have made it worse. So I ran into my room and crawled into bed.

"Show me where you got the nail," Daddy said, still standing.

Mama took the blanket off her legs to start to show him the foot.

"No, Jewell, I mean show me where the nail was when you stepped on it," he grinned.

Knowing she was unable to run from him, Mama got up and hobbled to the back kitchen door. She opened it and went into the furnace room assuming that Daddy would follow. Instead, Daddy shut the door locking her in the furnace room.

"You sleep in the furnace room tonight," Daddy smirked. "That'll teach you, trying to get somebody to feel sorry for you."

She started beating on the door. "Quinton, let me in! I can't stay out here all night! Please!"

Daddy turned his back and went into the bedroom, shutting the door to her pleas.

"Daddy, please let her come in!" I yelled from my bed.

"Go to sleep, Susan. She's got to learn," Daddy yelled back. "Don't you dare let her in!"

After a few minutes, it was quiet. Mama quit beating on the door. I waited a long time and then I sneaked out of bed. I peeked in to see Daddy asleep and then went to the back door and unlocked it for Mama. We didn't speak in the darkness. She leaned on me as I helped her into my bedroom. I tried not to move that night sleeping with her. I was afraid I would accidently hurt her foot.

The next day, Mama visited the doctor who bandaged her foot and gave her a tetanus shot. It didn't keep her from going to work. And, unfortunately, I went to school.

CHAPTER FIVE

Early on Thanksgiving morning, Mama and I sat at Granny's kitchen table, feeding whole cranberries into the cast iron grinder to make relish. Granny washed and dried the turkey, then rubbed it down with butter. After placing it in a large roasting pan, I helped cover the bird with aluminum foil. Finally, I held the oven door open while Mama and Granny managed to shove the pan inside the oven. Shuck beans cooked on one burner while Granny's garden frozen Silver Queen corn simmered on a back burner. In between washing dishes, Granny finished the relish as Mama rolled and cut the yeast-risen dough for dumplings, noodles, and hot rolls. A tray of a variety of radishes, black olives, green onions, and sweet pickles laid wrapped in a plastic wrap in the refrigerator along with the deviled eggs. A sweet potato casserole topped with marshmallows sat on the counter ready for the oven.

With a crumbled day-old pan of cornbread, hard-boiled eggs, chopped celery and onion, and a lot of sage, Mama prepared the dressing, except for the broth which would come from the cooked turkey. I watched. "Mama, how do you know how much sage to put in?" I asked, observing her measuring with her hands and fingers.

"You just know, that's all. I only measure when it's something I'm not used to making. Your Granny showed me how to make this dressing about when I was your age. It's a family recipe," Mama explained. "And it's a taste test way. By the time the broth is added to make it mushy, I taste it to see if I need to add more. Sometimes with that sage, I claim I stumped my toe pouring it in and that is why there's too much sage." Mama grinned and Granny laughed out loud.

"Aw, Mama, that's funny!" I said with a giggle.

After the turkey baked, Mama and Granny finished the rest of the fixings for the big Thanksgiving meal. "It's nearly eleven o'clock, we're right on time," Granny said, feeling satisfied with her work crew. Well, Mama's work at least.

There were chatter and clatter in Granny's kitchen, a happy feeling, one that I wished our house had. Mamas' sisters and their families were coming to Granny's house for the holiday meal. It was tradition. I never thought about the other sides of the families, like Daddy's people. I knew his father lived in an apartment in Harlan and his mother was never mentioned. And for some reason, I knew not to ask.

By the time, Mama's two sisters with their families and brother arrived, there was so much hugging and kissing that I hid in one of the bedrooms, dragging my cousin, Jane, with me. I could hardly stand being around all that love. Jane's mother brought a pumpkin pie and my favorite chocolate cake smothered in chocolate icing topped with pecans. Aunt Grace brought her famous homemade boiled custard and banana pudding.

The kitchen was filled with laughter as the women hurried to put the food on the fancy dining room table. Granny used her silver threaded brocade tablecloth with linen napkins and her best dishes. Orange tapered candles placed at each end of the table added to the festive atmosphere. Jane and I crawled under the table and watched the feet bringing the food into the dining room. We figured out whose feet belonged to which one. We thought it was funny.

The men, dressed in dark suits with ties, fled immediately to the living room to watch television or read the *Knoxville News Sentinel*. Polite conversation was exchanged as was expected.

On television, The Macy's Parade and football kept them occupied so they did not have to engage in much more than a Howdy-Do.

Hitchhiking from Loyall to Lawnvale, Daddy came through the back door just as the feast was ready. He hugged his sisters-in-law and mother-in-law, smiling and giving high praises for the wonderful aromas circulating the kitchen. He avoided hugging Mama but no one noticed. The charming man greeted his three brothers-in-law with such a pleasant attitude, I wondered if he was an imposter. When he found me under the table, I knew I had to pretend. Reluctantly, I hugged him. Dressed in his one dark blue suit, he smelled of Old Spice and Listerine. At least, it was an improvement.

Daddy hated the family gatherings. I heard him once tell Mama during a tirade that her sisters had married up but she had married down, that he was just a barber. It was true that her sisters lived more comfortably and had more advantages but Mama never gave it a thought. She was happy for them. All my Mama prayed for was peace.

Granny gave the call for everyone to come to the table. Since Granddaddy passed away, the head of the table went to Mama's oldest brother-in-law. Granny always sat at the other end of the large oak table. I never understood that but I did notice that if the brothers-in-law were not visiting, then the chair was given to Mama's brother. Daddy was never given the honor even though Granny clearly liked him.

After Granny said the blessing, the food was passed around as if we hadn't eaten a meal in a month. But that is how Granny measured her worth. The food had to be enjoyed or her feelings were hurt . . . and we didn't want to disappoint Granny. I ate so fast my stomach hurt. Jane picked at her food as usual so I ate her buttered roll right off her plate. She didn't care. She ate like a bird as much as I ate like a starved puppy. Yet, we were both little and boney.

As soon as dessert was to be served, Daddy announced that he was going up to Harlan to see his father. He pushed back his chair, stood up and told everyone how good it was to see them. He went over and kissed Granny on the cheek and thanked her for the food. Granny asked if he wanted to take a plate of food to his father but Daddy declined saying he was hitchhiking and couldn't carry it. He said his father was eating with some friends at the Llewelyn Hotel. He shook hands with his brothers-in-law and left out the front door. Finished with my plate of food, I quickly excused myself and went into the living room. From a window, I watched Daddy stand on the side of the highway to catch a ride. I was right! A car stopped and picked him up but it was headed back down to our house, not toward Harlan. I knew he was lying. At least he didn't embarrass Mama.

At the mention of chocolate cake, I rejoined the family. Mama cut the cake and dished out the pudding while her sisters served us, Granny being served a piece of pumpkin pie first, of course. The faces around the table looked almost painful as our stomachs were already abundantly satisfied. It was just too good to stop.

Then a knock at the front door surprised all of us. Mama opened the door to see five year old Mikey, a neighborhood boy, standing in front of her. Panting for breath and waving his arms, he spoke so fast she couldn't understand him.

"Mikey, slow down and tell me again. I don't know what you're talking about," Mama said. "What is wrong? Is your mother okay?"

Mikey took a deep breath. "It's your car! It's gone. I saw them! Look!" Mikey screamed and pointed to where the car had been parked. "My mother said to tell you to call the police!"

Mama's eyes got big as saucers as she looked out to see her car gone. Everyone at the table rushed to the windows. Sure enough, it had been stolen. Mama called the State Police who came quickly and talked to Mikey, taking his description of the boy and girl who drove off in Mama's car. Fortunately, the police found the old Ford just a few miles from Granny's house and brought the two suspects back for Mikey to identify. Instead, the two admitted to the theft and said they were sorry. Mama felt compassion for the two teenagers and chose not to file charges. After all, it was Thanksgiving.

Just as everyone settled down in the living room, the table cleared and the dishes washed, the phone rang. Mama answered.

"When are you coming home? The fire's out and the house is cold. Get down here right now," Daddy screamed over the phone. "I'm hungry. Bring me something to eat."

I walked into the kitchen where my mother was on the phone. I could see her face turn pale; her hand shook while holding the receiver.

"All right, Quinton, we'll be home in a few minutes," Mama told him before hanging up the phone.

I didn't bother asking if I could stay at Granny's. I knew my fun time was over and, besides, I couldn't leave my mother alone. Mama fixed a plate of food for Daddy. We made our apologies for leaving early, hugged and kissed all the relatives, and headed back to Loyall where evil waited.

I was grateful it was nearly dark when we got home. As soon as we walked inside, Mama and I pulled the curtains together in all windows, hoping to stifle the noise and the scenes inside our house. Although the television was blaring, Daddy sat motionless in his chair, eyes closed, drooling out of the side of his mouth. We slipped silently into the kitchen, not daring to look directly at him.

First, Mama filled the furnace and built a fire. In no time, the house was warm. As she turned the automatic washer on, she whispered, "Susan, it's supposed to get in the twenties tomorrow night so I'm going ahead and wash a load of clothes now. I don't want to take a chance of the pipes freezing. We've been lucky so far. Why don't you stay in here and keep me company?"

I nodded. It was too early to go to bed and didn't want to sit in the same room with Daddy. So Mama and I sat at the table and looked in the pages of the Sears and Roebuck catalog. I was only interested in the toys since Christmas was a month away. As the washer kicked into the spin cycle, a loud noise caused us to jump. She stopped the washer and opened the lid. I peeked into the living room, Daddy still slept. She rearranged the wet clothes to balance the tub and started the spin cycle again. Afterwards, we hung the clothes to dry on a clothesline strung in the bathroom. The heat from the registers would dry the clothes by morning. Although inconvenient, dodging wet clothes, it was the only way to dry them in the winter.

By ten o'clock, both of us were ready to go to bed. It had been a long day. We decided to leave Daddy in his chair. When Mama turned the television off, he didn't budge. As she tucked me into bed, she whispered, "Honey, there's no need to say anything about the car being stolen today. Do you understand?"

"Yes, Mama," I replied, knowing that if Daddy knew, he would blame Mama.

I must have slept through part of it because Mama was in the kitchen with Daddy when I heard her screaming. It showed three a.m. on my alarm clock. I smelled smoke.

"Stop, Quinton! You're going to set the house on fire!" Mama hollered, a real panic in her voice. "You're crazy!"

"Get those damn clothes out of my way! I'll burn every one of them up!" Daddy roared.

I crawled out of bed and ran into the bathroom in time to see Mama grabbing one of her flaming blouses off the clothesline and throw it in the bathtub. Two other blouses were smoldering, ruined by burnt holes from Daddy's lighter.

I pulled the lighter out of his hand as he just stood there while Mama ran water on the tub to put the fire out. It was as if he was watching a movie, no visible emotion. He looked at me, turned and went back in the living room to his chair.

"Oh, Susan, my clothes, he burned my clothes!" Mama sobbed. "I just can hardly stand this."

I hugged my mother, not knowing what else to do. I took the damaged wet clothes and put them in the garbage. My poor mother sat on the edge of the tub, bent over with her face in her hands, and cried. Noticing the quiet from Daddy, I peeked into the living room. He wasn't there. He had gone to bed. With only a couple of hours before morning, Mama and I stayed in the kitchen waiting for daybreak. She sat on a stool, looking out a window, drinking coffee and chain-smoking. I wished she would look at me or talk to me but her thoughts were in a world I didn't belong.

It was Friday, the day after Thanksgiving, no school. By eight a.m., I was at Granny's house and Mama was at work. I grabbed a pillow and fell asleep on the couch, waking up three hours later. I felt Granny putting her hand on my forehead, probably thinking I was getting sick. I was . . . sick of everything in my life, sick of Daddy, sick of secrets, just plain sick.

"Here, Susan, you better wake up. It's nearly lunchtime. Come on in the kitchen. I heated up some turkey and noodles," Granny said softly, stroking my hair.

I stretched out on the couch and rubbed my eyes. "Okay. I think I could stretch a country mile and walk back."

I followed Granny and the wonderful aroma of another Thanksgiving meal into the kitchen. We ate slowly, savoring every bite. Granny was a big eater but thin as a rail. Of course, the only time she sat down was to eat. She believed in work and expected no less from everyone else.

"What is Santa Claus going to bring you this year?" Granny asked, after wiping her mouth with a napkin.

"Aw, Granny, I know there isn't a Santa Claus! What I really want is one of those Madame Alexander dolls. I think I am getting too big for dolls so I've decided that this year will be my last doll. I'm growing up, you know. If I got that doll, I wouldn't play with it. I would put it up and save it until I got really old, like thirty," I answered.

"Are you sure?" Granny asked, surprised by the revelation that her little granddaughter had such grown up thoughts.

"Well, that's what I'm thinking right now but I can always change my mind," I informed her. "My friend, Dottie, changes her mind all the time. I never know what she's thinking. Just like she said she wanted a record player for Christmas and now she doesn't. I don't know why because she sure likes to play with mine when she comes to my house."

Granny nodded and listened as I rambled on about everything and nothing. It felt good to talk, as if what I said was important.

When Mama and I arrived home that afternoon, Daddy was gone. Although the weather was cold, it was apparent, with the fishing gear gone, that Daddy went to Norris Lake again. Sometimes, good things happened. *Maybe he'll drown*, I thought briefly as I took a bath that night. *Maybe he will get drunk and fall in the lake.*

With the night being our own, we went to bed early, still exhausted from the night before. I got to sleep in my bed alone, stretching my arms out to the sides, rubbing my feet up and down between the sheets. It was a happy feeling. As I settled down to say my prayers, I suddenly felt ashamed. I prayed that God forgives me for having bad thoughts about Daddy. I knew it was wrong but such a powerful urge to hate him kept me from loving him. Also, I was afraid the priest was going to get tired of me repeating my sins.

The weeks went by too fast and Christmas Holidays seemed to appear magically. Although Daddy still ranted and raved nearly every night, I knew it could have been worse. Two days before Christmas Eve, Daddy showed up at my school with ice cream treats, as if to buy my love. I didn't care and it made me mad for the nuns to applaud him. *If they only knew*, I thought.

51

On the Saturday evening before Christmas, Mama and I went to town to see the Christmas parade. There were several high school bands, dressed in their woolen uniforms, playing Christmas carols, marching down Central Street in front of the courthouse. The wintry night air gave chill bumps and red noses to the majorettes wearing their short costumes. The floats carried kings and queens, boy scouts, and church groups. At the end of the parade was the big red fire truck with its blaring siren. Santa Claus sat on top, throwing hard candy out to the crowds. Daddy was nowhere to be seen.

Three days before Christmas, Mama bought our tree, a five-foot pine. It hung out of the trunk of the car, nearly dragging the ground. She had a rope tied from the trunk lid to the back bumper to keep the tree from falling out. I held my breath as she parked in front of Granny's house to get me after school. We wasted no time getting home before dark. I helped her gently pull it out of the trunk and carry it into the house.

"Honey, be careful with the branches. We don't want the pine needles falling off before Christmas. You know what a mess it makes!" she said, examining her choice. "Isn't it a nice one?"

"Yes, Mama," I said, trying to tip and hold up the tree trunk while Mama slipped the tree stand under it.

With the tree down in the holder, Mama poured a little water in it and two baby aspirins. We decorated the tree with multi-colored lights, balls, and lots of tinsel. It was the prettiest tree we ever had. The smell of pine was exhilarating, giving thoughts of carols, cookies, hot chocolate, and Santa Claus. I knew there wasn't a real Santa but I loved to imagine that just maybe . . .

After setting the star on top of the tree, we sat down to admire our handiwork. Then we wrapped a folded white sheet around the base of the tree, spreading it out to make a circle. I put the manger on the sheet under the tree along with my little book, "Twas the Night Before Christmas." I thought the tree looked very fancy, like what the rich people on Ivy Hill might have.

For the next two nights, Daddy never even acknowledged the tree standing in the corner of the living room. In fact, he was very quiet. He came home before midnight, sat in his chair staring at television until the stations went off the air, and went to bed. He kept his bottle of whiskey in the floor beside his chair. He just didn't talk, not to Mama, not to me. She stayed in the kitchen while I stayed in my room. It was strange.

On Christmas Eve, school let out early. Dottie's mother dropped me off at Granny's. It was strange to get out of school in the middle of the week. Granny had her decorated tree placed in front of the living room window so a passerby might admire it.

"Granny, your tree is really pretty. Where did you get it?" I asked.

"Why, honey, your Daddy brought it to me. I thought you knew," she said.

"Oh, I forgot," I said, so shocked that no other words came to mind.

"Quinton and his fishing buddy brought it to me yesterday in a truck. It was such a nice surprise. I wasn't going to put one up this year and I told your Mama not to get me one," Granny explained. "You sure do have a good Daddy."

Not able to respond to that, I smiled. I sat in the living room admiring Granny's pine tree, trying to figure out what Daddy was up to. When Mama came to pick me up, the look on her face was pure shock and confusion. We left before Granny caught onto our acting. On the way home, Mama didn't say a word.

Even though waiting up to go to Midnight Mass on Christmas Eve was a long ritual, I really enjoyed the anticipation. After supper, we took our baths and laid our dresses out on the bed for later. Then Mama made some sugar cookies for Santa's plate. We each ate three, leaving four for Santa. Mama stashed the rest of the cookies wrapped in aluminum foil in the cookie

53

jar. Daddy came home later, took a bath, and put his suit on. I thought maybe he would bring presents, but no. I didn't have any money to buy presents for Mama or anyone else. It looked so bare under the tree.

"Do you want something to eat?" Mama asked him, hoping food in his stomach would sober him up.

He shook his head, not even looking at her. His attention was a program on television. She knew to leave him alone.

Mama and I dressed in our finest. She looked beautiful in her red dress with a small veiled hat to match. I thought my black velvet dress with satin collar and bow made me almost pretty. My soft velvet tam lay just perfect, not messing up my hair. This was the only time I enjoyed dressing up. I looked out the window into the darkness about eleven p.m. and found a winter wonderland. Only a couple of inches of fresh snow, it gave a clean and renewed sense of hope. "Mama, it's snowed! Look outside!" I hollered as I opened the front door.

Daddy jumped up. "Jewell, I guess we better go if the roads are getting bad," he said. "I'll go out and warm the car up."

Mama and I didn't say anything. We were too afraid to break the spell that came over Daddy. We didn't know what was going on with him but this was Christmas and we were grateful for anything close to normal.

The ride to church was slow, Daddy driving very carefully. No one spoke. I sat in between Daddy and Mama in the front seat. It was a tight fit but I hated sitting in the back seat alone. The church was nearly full when we got there. Luckily, we found room in the third pew from the back, which was usually where we sat anyway. I did a tiny wave at Dottie and her family across the aisle. She smiled back, her white teeth gleaming.

The Latin Mass was beautiful even if most of us didn't know what we were saying. The choir sang several carols, including "Oh Holy Night," one of Mama's favorites. But when a lady named Joyce sang "Ave Maria" toward the end of the service,

Mama's eyes filled with tears. She reached in her purse for a tissue. Daddy gave her a stern look.

After church, while several stood out in the cold and snow wishing everyone a Merry Christmas, Mama and I knelt at the altar in front of the manger display and said a little prayer. I didn't ask what to pray for, I just prayed. When we walked out of church, we found Daddy shaking hands with nearly everyone, laughing and talking up a good time. Mama joined a group of women chatting about how much was spent on presents that year. Dottie and I snickered and giggled, the excitement of Christmas morning was near.

When we got home, I quickly put my pajamas on and placed the plate of cookies and glass of milk on an end table next to the Christmas tree. I sat in a chair, mesmerized by the lights and glitter. I felt it was going to be the greatest Christmas we ever had. I was wrong. After Mama put on her nightclothes and filled the furnace, she sat in the kitchen smoking a cigarette. Daddy hung his suit up and put his pajama bottoms on. It appeared that he was going to bed.

"Quinton, aren't you going to put any presents under the tree for Susan?" Mama asked, not knowing what he planned.

Daddy turned with a jolt, nearly leaping at Mama like a tiger. He grabbed her by her pajama top and slung her against the stove, making a terrible metal thud. Before I could get into the kitchen, he pulled her by her hair into the living room.

"You see this?" Daddy yelled, pointing to the tree with one hand and nodding Mama's head with his hand full of hair. "Merry Christmas!"

In an instant, he flung her into the Christmas tree, causing it to fall on top of her. Light bulbs popped and the balls cracked. She didn't move. Daddy laughed. Then he noticed me standing there almost in a trance.

"Get your mother up," he ordered. "I'm going to bed."

I pulled the tree off of her and got the pine needles out of her hair as she sat in the floor. We set the tree upright and tried to rearrange the mess. The lights were ruined and most of the balls were shattered. There was nothing we could do. She slept with me that night.

When I woke the next morning, I had nearly forgot it was Christmas. I bounded out of bed and ran into the living room. Underneath the poor pitiful Christmas tree, I found my dream gift, a Madame Alexander Doll, dressed is so much finery that I could hardly find her shoes. She was the most beautiful doll in the world and I was going to keep her forever. To my delight, there was another present, one that I had wished for but never said anything about it. Or I didn't think I had. It was a Brownie camera. We never had a camera before. Also, I found coloring books and a big box of crayons, and paper dolls.

Mama stood in the doorway and watched me. "I guess Santa thought you were a good girl this year," she said.

"Oh, Mama, just look at all the stuff. Come and look at my doll. I just love her," I exclaimed, while pointing to three presents off to the side. "Whose are these?"

"They're for your Daddy . . . when he gets up," she answered.

There were no presents under the tree for my mother. My heart ached with sadness that I didn't get her anything for Christmas. I didn't open my mouth, even when Daddy opened his presents later. I hurt so badly for her. I promised myself that I was going to save every nickel and dime I got and buy my mother a present next Christmas, something fancy.

CHAPTER SIX

The next couple of years failed to bring any kind of family peace no matter how hard I prayed. It became more difficult to hide the chaos in my life. I felt so helpless watching my mother shrink away from everyone, including me. I begged her to leave but her answer was always the same, "Now, Susan, we can't leave because there is no place to go. Besides, there is no divorce for Catholics." When I dared to ask why God would want her to be in so much pain, Mama thought I was questioning God's plan.

At age eleven, I mastered the art of pretending, confident that no one knew of our nightmares. It seemed that the towns-people saw a different side of Daddy which caused me to scream inside. I couldn't understand the two sides of my father. *What did Mama and me do to deserve this*, I often thought. It was springtime when Daddy went on a three-night tirade, wanting Mama and me to move to Lexington. He insisted that he could make a lot of money in the city and that all his problems would disappear if we got out of Harlan. When she refused to give up her job and leave, Daddy blamed Granny, that Mama wouldn't leave her mother. Enraged of this thought, Daddy began a verbal attack about Granny, eventually blaming everything on her.

Mama just let him rant on . . . until one day soon after the tirade he called her at work and threatened to go to Granny's house. This time she really feared him, not for her sake but for Granny. She called Granny and told her that Daddy was drunk.

They decided that we would spend the night at Bays Motel. When Dottie's mother dropped me off at Granny's from school, Granny didn't tell me anything but I could see that something was wrong. I looked in a paper sack that Granny placed at the back door. It was filled with clothes and a hair brush. Within a few minutes, Mama arrived. She was early.

"Susan, your Daddy has been drinking so we are going to spend the night at a motel," Mama said softly.

"But, Mama, I don't have any clothes for school tomorrow," I whined.

"Don't worry. I'll hang your clothes up when we get to the room. It'll be just fine. You can wear them again tomorrow," Mama answered, brushing her hand gently over my hair.

Then Mama turned toward Granny, unable to look at her directly in the face. "Mother, are you ready?"

"Yes, let me lock the front door and we can go out the back," Granny replied.

After Granny checked each room, grabbed her sack of clothes, and locked the doors, we began the drive to Bays Motel.

"What about your brother?" Granny asked, breaking the silence.

"We're going by the hospital and I'll tell him where we will be. If he wants to come to the motel room after work, then I can get him a room," Mama explained.

Mama drove around to the side of the hospital at the loading dock and parked. Granny and I stayed inside the car while Mama asked somebody to get her brother. I watched but couldn't hear the conversation between my mother and my uncle. After Mama returned to the car, she told Granny not to worry, that he was going to stay overnight at the hospital.

At the motel, our room had twin beds, one for Granny and one for Mama and me. It wasn't home but it had a television.

"Honey, I'm going to the restaurant across the highway and get us something to eat. You stay here and keep Granny company," Mama said, peeking out the door as if expecting Daddy to be lurking in the bushes.

I nodded. After stacking my school books on the small desk beside a bed, I turned the television on and adjusted the tuner to get a better picture. Granny was quiet, sitting on the edge of her bed with her hands folded in her lap. Her face was pale, a blank expression that kinda scared me.

"Granny, do you want me to run the channels? Maybe we can find the news," I suggested. I hated watching the evening news but I thought that would cheer her up.

"No, honey, but you watch whatever you want. I'm just fine," Granny said.

Within thirty minutes, Mama was back carrying hamburgers, french fries, a milkshake for me, and coffee for her and Granny. I was beginning to enjoy this little stay at the motel. The food was good; the atmosphere was so tense and silent that I had to turn the volume down on the television twice. I didn't know if Mama was worried or embarrassed since this was the first time Mama ever admitted to Granny that Daddy might be violent.

Granny pulled the clothes out of her sack. "Here, Susan, I brought you this to wear," she said, handing me the fresh cotton nightgown. "It might be a little big on you but it doesn't matter."

"Go on in the bathroom, take a bath and put it on. I'll hang your clothes up in the bathroom and the steam from the hot water will take most of the wrinkles out," Mama said.

"Okay, Mama," I replied. "Do I still have to do my homework?"

"Of course. You can do it after you get ready for bed. If you need help, I'll try," Mama answered.

While I was in the bathroom, I could hear them talking but their conversation was in a near whisper. I filled the claw bathtub with at least four inches and enjoyed the freedom of water. Mama knocked on the door twice before I gave up, pulled the stopper, allowing the water to suck down the drain. After drying on a large white towel and putting on the oversized gown, I took a wet washcloth and rubbed my teeth. As soon as I opened the door back into the room, Mama rushed in, grabbed my clothes and hung them on a wire coat hanger over the towel bar. The hot mist in the bathroom was as thick as fog.

While I finished my homework, Granny took a bath, then Mama. Granny had brought a nightgown for Mama but she refused. My mother sat by the window moving the heavy curtain ever so slightly to peek out, keeping watch. Although I didn't say anything, I couldn't understand what she expected. The motel was off the main road. Daddy didn't have a car, and he didn't know where we were. I just didn't see a problem.

That night, I snuggled down in my twin bed as Granny pulled the covers up to her chin in her bed. Her snoring started began almost immediately. She always said she could sleep through a tornado. But she didn't know how much damage a human tornado could do. Mama turned off the television about nine o'clock, then the lamp beside my bed. Leaving her in the dark, I asked, "Mama, aren't you coming to bed?"

"No, I'm not sleepy. You close your eyes. I'm going to sit up awhile," Mama whispered as she put another cigarette out in the overflowing ashtray. "I'll come to bed later."

I woke several times that night, only to see my mother's silhouette staring out the window. I prayed that she would come to bed . . . but she didn't.

As the morning sun made a stream of rays between the curtains onto my bed, I watched layers of cigarette smoke float like ocean waves. When Mama disturbed the scene, the layers exploded into clouds, disappearing . . . just as I wished I could have. But then, who would take care of Mama?

By seven a.m., Granny was already up, dressed, and drinking coffee that Mama had brought in from somewhere. I jumped out of bed and ran into the bathroom. Sure enough, my clothes didn't have very many wrinkles in them. I dressed quickly.

"Susan, there's a donut out here for you," Mama said. "I went out early. And here's a little carton of milk."

It was such a treat to get a donut that I didn't mind drinking the milk, although I would have preferred chocolate milk. Neither Granny nor Mama said much. As we got into the car, I panicked. "Mama, what about Dottie and her sister? How are they going to get to school?"

"Don't worry, I called Dottie's mother yesterday and told her I couldn't pick them up this morning," Mama explained. "So after today, things will get back to normal now."

Sitting in the front seat between the two most important people in my life, looking out the front windshield at the beautiful green mountains surrounding me, I wondered, *What is normal?*

My day at school was uneventful. Dottie asked me what happened and I couldn't think of anything to tell her so I just shrugged my shoulders. She looked at me, rolled her eyes, and shook her head. I knew that if I lied, then I would have to confess it to the priest. And I was bound by my promise to my mother not to tell anyone our troubles. I hated looking stupid but that was my only choice.

At Granny's house after school, nothing was mentioned about our night at Bays Motel. While Granny worked in her garden, I sat in the living room and watched television until Mama came. After a brief exchange of almost strange pleasantries between Granny and Mama, we went home. Daddy wasn't there.

While Mama fixed supper, I spread my books out on the kitchen table and did my homework. It was easier to think when Daddy wasn't there. We ate quietly. Mama pushed her food around in her plate, taking a nibble or two. I ate hungrily as if food would solve all my problems.

"Where's Daddy?" I asked, stabbing the fork into my piece of meatloaf forcefully.

"I don't know. He called me right before I got off of work, said some things and hung up," she said "I don't want to talk about it."

So we didn't . . . talk about it. After supper, we sat out on the porch, a cool spring rain driving us inside after a few minutes. Nighttime came too quickly. Our routine of preparation for the unknown seemed useless. We went to bed early. Daddy didn't come home that night.

At breakfast, I watched as Mama rushed around the kitchen in a flurry, almost in a happy state. Before I caught myself, the words just blurted out of my mouth like a bursting dam. "Maybe Daddy got killed last night!"

She turned with a jerk, looked directly at my hopeful face and said, "Don't you ever say that again!"

Shocked at her reaction, I wondered how she could take up for the man who beat her mercilessly and made out lives so miserable. My mouth flew open again. "Mama, please let's run away."

"I have told you time and time again, I can't leave. There is not one divorce in my family and besides we're Catholic," she insisted. "Now get your things. It's time to go to school."

That night, Daddy came home with a new agenda. He wanted to take me fishing at Norris Lake in Tennessee on Saturday. I had never asked to go with him before and had no desire to be with him all day. I figured Mama would never allow him to take me that far away from home, but I was wrong. By the time Daddy finished twisting her arm behind her back and pulling her head back by her hair, she agreed. He thanked her and went to bed.

For the next two days, I prayed so hard that God would do something to stop me from going to the lake. I would have even settled for a broken leg or something. Daddy had taken me fishing at the Cumberland River many times but this was different. There was no where to run if Daddy got crazy and I didn't know how to get back home. I should have told Mama I didn't want to go but then it would have been so bad for her. Daddy seemed anxious for Saturday to arrive. He told the owner of the barbershop that he needed to take off work. It really didn't matter to the owner. Daddy's behavior at home was tolerable, coming home late as usual but going straight to bed.

Early Saturday morning, Daddy put his fishing gear in the trunk while I helped Mama to pack a lunch. I thought I heard a small doubt in her voice as she told me to be careful, like she really didn't want me to go, that maybe she made a mistake letting me go. I didn't know what to say so I told her I would be just fine and not to worry. I figured it couldn't be any worse than what I was used to.

She stood on the porch as we started to leave. "Quinton, you bring her back all in one piece, you hear me!" Mama exclaimed. "Don't you drive fast either!"

Daddy ignored her and slide into the driver's seat. I hugged and kissed my mother before joining Daddy in the car. I had never heard Mama give Daddy orders like that and I liked it. I rolled down the window and waved as we rode away.

As we traveled the winding two lane roads with hairpin curves and weaving around nearly unavoidable potholes, I clutched the armrest to keep me from hitting the dashboard. Daddy was in a hurry.

"Daddy, slow down a little. You're pushing me all over the seat!" I complained.

"Okay, sorry about that," he answered, raising his foot off the accelerator a bit to slow the speed. "You know, we're going to have a really big time today. We'll rent us a runabout at the dock, with a trolling motor. That's all we'll need since you don't like going fast. But first, I need to stop at a store in Cumberland Gap for just a minute and buy me a pack of cigarettes. It won't take long."

After more than an hour of driving, Daddy pulled up in front of a small unpainted store with a wooden porch. The window was covered with stickers and signs, making it impossible to see inside. I didn't like that place.

"Stay in the car, honey. I'll be back in a few minutes. Do you want any candy?" he asked, turning the motor off.

"Can't I go with you?" I asked. "I won't buy anything."

"No, little girls can't go in there. I'll be right back," he said. "Roll the window up and lock the door."

I did what I was told. Daddy did come back in a few minutes carrying a small brown sack. He handed me a pack of Sugar Babies and put the sack in the back seat.

Then we started the drive up the Cumberland Gap mountain, a huge mountain that touched the sky. The old Ford hugged the road as I looked out and straight down into the deep brush-covered ravines. One tiny mistake, a tremor of Daddy's hand, would careen the car over the mountain into the Gap below. At the top, on the left against the mountain was Cudjo's Cave and on my right, nearly hanging over the edge, was a novelty store. Daddy had to slow down to a crawl. Several cars were parked off the side of the road as visitors mingled inside and outside the tiny building. A totem pole stood beside the doorway while hanging wind chimes tinkled and clanged.

"Remember the bow and arrow I brought you one time?" he asked. "Well, that is where I got it. If you're a good girl, I might just stop there on our way back home. I know you like Indian toys and they have shelves of them."

Although I was eleven years old, I still enjoyed a toy from time to time. Also, after writing a report on the Cherokee for a school project, I became fascinated with Indians. "Oh, yes, Daddy, I'll be good!" I yelled, determined to make the best out of my situation.

By the time we got to the lake, parked the car, carried everything down to the dock, rented a boat, and started out into the channel, it was close to lunchtime. I sat in front while he steered the motor, turning this way and that, eventually dropping the small anchor in a cove not far from 33 Bridge Boat Dock.

"Here, Susan, bait your hook," he said, handing me a cup of worms he had bought at the dock. "These look good, big and fat."

I grabbed one of the slimy worms, baited, and cast my line as far as I could. "Daddy, I'm hungry. Do you want a sandwich?" I asked, wiping my hands on my shirt before getting into the lunch sack.

"No, I'm not hungry but I think I'll get something to drink," Daddy answered, pulling a half pint of whiskey out of the bag he bought in Cumberland Gap. With one quick move, he opened the bottle, turned it up, and took a long gurgling swallow. Then, making a screwed up face, he ordered, "Don't tell your mother."

I just stared at him. *How could he do this? What was I going to do if he got mean? I can't swim that far. I can't drive a car.*

It was a good thing that silence beckoned when we fished. My thoughts rambled so badly that I turned my head as tears blurred my sight. I pretended to rub my face to wipe my eyes. Suddenly, I wasn't hungry. Daddy seemed to enjoy himself, having his daughter with him on the lake, fishing, no stress, no worries. Just me, him, and the bottle.

By late afternoon, we caught a stringer of fish, mostly bluegills. Although there was plenty of daylight still ahead, the sun was lowering behind the mountains.

"I guess it's time to head back to the dock, Daddy," I suggested, really feeling tired and wanting to go home.

Daddy finished his second half pint and stuck the empty bottle back into the paper sack. "Okay, I guess you're right, just like you mother," he uttered as he released the stringer of fish back into the water. "Here, change places with me. You might as well learn how to steer the boat. It ain't hard."

We changed places so that I sat in the back next to the motor. He gave simple instructions and I followed them, afraid not to. Actually, it really wasn't hard to guide the boat. I was having a good time . . . until the motor quit several yards before we got to land. The dock was in our sight so I knew we weren't lost. Daddy thought at first I flooded the motor but soon discovered it was not my fault.

"Susan, we are going to have to paddle to the dock. There's no other way," Daddy said, giving me one of the paddles in the aluminum boat. "You stay in the back of the boat to paddle and I'll paddle in the front. If you see another boat, wave and holler at them. Maybe they'll come over and tow us to the dock."

Daddy paddled fiercely. I didn't know if it was because he was angry or drunk. No one came by to help us so it took more than an hour to arrive at the dock. Daddy's clothes were drenched by sweat. My hair stuck to my head like a wet dog. Hurriedly, we loaded the car and began our trip home.

Out of nowhere, he changed. Between his drunken laughter and reckless driving, I was terrified sitting in the front seat. He passed cars on curves going up the mountain, once dipping off the road into a small ditch and bouncing back onto the road, nearly hitting an oncoming car.

"Daddy, I'm sleepy. I'm getting in the back," I hollered, quickly crawling over the top of the front seat and laying down on the back seat.

I figured that if we went off the mountain, then maybe since I was in the back, I wouldn't get killed. The weaving and dodging movement made me nauseous. I grabbed the lunch sack and threw up in it. Daddy didn't even notice.

Suddenly, we stopped. I was afraid to raise my aching head, not knowing what to expect.

"We're here, honey. Come on and get out," Daddy said, opening his door.

"We're home?" I asked.

"No, I told you if you were good, I'd buy you something. We're here at the Cudjo Cave Store," he answered. "Come on, we don't have all day."

Slowly, we got out of the car. With Daddy weaving and me stumbling, we looked like a couple of drunks. Inside the store, I was amazed by the hundreds of trinkets, toys, knickknacks, and Indian novelties. I chose a small Indian doll, with long black braided hair, wearing a tan Indian dress. She had a tiny beaded headband and moccasins on her feet. I loved her.

As Daddy pulled back onto the road, I begged, "Please don't drive so fast. It scares me."

He took his eyes off the road, staring at me sitting beside him. "Just like your mother!" he spouted, angrily.

Yet, he did slow down. We didn't speak until we were almost home. I didn't care. I didn't have anything to talk to him about and I could see that the closer we got home, the meaner he looked. Being with him today gave my mother a chance to rest and, of course, I got my doll.

Mama was so happy to see me and I was awful glad to be home. She whispered in my ear that she would never do that to me again. I told her it was okay. Daddy unloaded the car, never saying anything about the vomit in the sack. I guess he didn't want her to know. Unusually quiet, Daddy sat in front of the television, comforted by his third bottle of booze. Mama and I sat in the kitchen while I told her about my exciting day. Daddy went to bed early. Tomorrow was Sunday Mass.

CHAPTER SEVEN

After eighth grade graduation from Holy Trinity, I looked forward to going to high school. I wasn't prepared for changing classes, long hallways to the unknown, and the hundreds of students. Although the Loyall High School was half a block from our house, Mama enrolled me at the Harlan City School. Her reasoning was that since she worked in town, I could walk to her office after school. If I had gone to Loyall, I would have been home alone after school. The saddest part was not having my best friend with me. Since Dottie was a year younger, I felt like life was pulling me away from her. She was the only sane person in my life at the time. And even when she graduated, she would attend Loyall. But my future was not of my choosing so I accepted the fact that I was going to enroll at Harlan High School because that was what my mother wanted. Of course, I still had the summer to enjoy before that happened.

The Loyall Youth Center was the focal point to meet friends, dance, and play ping-pong. The summer I turned fourteen, Dottie and I went to the youth center every Friday and Saturday night. We had discovered boys. My heart skipped a beat every time one certain boy, his brother, and his friends from Sukey Ridge stood at the front door of the center paying a dime to get inside.

"Oh God, Dottie, there they are," I whispered, my hand cupped over my mouth.

"Okay, I'm going to walk by them and you come up to me like you are going to tell me something," Dottie planned, inching away.

I did follow her as she tried to make eye contact with one of the boys. It didn't work. The boys walked by and huddled in the back of the room where the jukebox played "Sugar Shack." Dottie and I took turns standing at the jukebox so we could just catch a look. I was in love but he didn't know I was alive. There were so many beautiful girls in there with perfect hair, perfect figures, expensive clothes, and most of all none wore coke-bottle glasses like mine.

That night when the center closed, Dottie and I started to turn the corner to walk the half block to my house. I heard a voice, "Where are you going?" I turned around to face the boy, about six inches away from me. I hollered.

"Good grief, I ain't that bad, am I?" he said with a grin.

"Uh, no, I'm sorry. We're going home. I mean, going to my house, around the corner," I stumbled with the words so badly that I choked.

"Well, can we walk you two home?" he asked and pointed back to his brother standing by the fire hydrant.

"Sure," Dottie and I said in unison.

As we all walked in the middle of the road at nine o'clock at night, I thought, *Oh God, please don't let Daddy be home. Please, please, please.*

Turning the corner, I noticed that the porch light was off. That was a signal to me that Daddy was home. My heart broke. I stopped across the street in front of my house.

"Hey, I don't mind walking you to the porch," he said. "Is your old man home or something?"

Dottie looked at me wild-eyed and confused.

"Yeah, that's it. But thanks for walking us. Maybe, we'll see you next week," I said quickly and grabbed Dottie, pulling her along across the street.

The boys just laughed and disappeared into the night.

Dottie was furious with me. "Look, I don't know what is wrong with you but you just missed out on the best time of your life," Dottie grumbled. "And I was going to get kissed, I just know it."

Standing on the porch in the dark, I confessed, "Look, Dottie, I'm sorry but I don't know what's going on in my house. I didn't know Daddy was going to be home an . . . " I apologized. "Can you walk on down to your house by yourself? I'll explain later, I promise."

"Sure, sure, Call me tomorrow," Dottie pouted, leaving in a huff. "I swear you'd better think of something good because I am really mad right now."

"Do you want me to walk you to the bridge?" I asked, hoping she'd say no.

"No, I'm not afraid," she answered. "We'll talk tomorrow. Bye."

I stood on the porch until she turned the corner to get back to the main road. I wasn't worried about her. Everybody strolled safely at all hours of the night in Loyall. But what went on behind closed doors presented a different scenario. I was going to have to tell Dottie about Daddy and I was going to do it tomorrow. It was just getting too hard.

I opened the unlocked front door, being met with yelling from the kitchen. "I'm home!" I hollered, hoping that Daddy would think Dottie was with me and be embarrassed. I was wrong.

"Come on in here, Susan. We've got to tell you something," Daddy hollered back.

I continued into the kitchen to find my mother sitting at the table with a half empty glass of whiskey in front of her. She appeared frightful with her hair in disarray, her hands shaking. Daddy, on the other hand, just had the half pint nearly empty placed in front of him. His face flushed, his eyes filled with excitement. *What was going on now*, I wondered as I sat down to hear the news.

"Is Dottie with you?" Mama asked.

"No, she went on home," I answered, glancing around the room to anticipate the unexpected.

"Okay, here's the deal. Your mother and I have decided that I am going to go to Lexington and work. I have a chance to buy a barbershop up there and make all kinds of money. You and your mother will stay here. I'm going to ride the Greyhound and come home every weekend. In the summer you can come visit me too," Daddy explained, his voice growing louder. "What do you think about that?"

I was shocked, nearly speechless. I quickly answered, fearing that the moment would be lost forever if I didn't approve. "Daddy, I think that's fine."

"Good, then it's settled. I'm going to bed," Daddy announced happily as he pushed his chair back, got up and stumbled to the bedroom.

I was numb. *Did I just hear him right? He's leaving. He's really going. Oh thank you God. Is this real? Oh God, please don't let him change his mind,* I prayed. I looked at my mother who in turn was staring at me. I couldn't tell what she was thinking. *Surely to goodness, she is glad. Why does she look so sad? How can she care what he does? Why doesn't she say anything?*

Finally, Mama spoke, "I think it's time for you to go to bed. Did you and Dottie have a good time tonight?"

I got up, went around to her, hugged her frail body and kissed the top of her head. "Yes, Mama, we had a good time," I answered. *Oh, thank you God!*

Watching Mama, it was as if that whole conversation with Daddy never happened. I left Mama sitting in the kitchen. She hardly ever went to bed before midnight and I just couldn't hold my eyes open any longer. Besides, I had a lot of thinking to do and I did that best laying in my own bed. Questions swirled in my mind that night with no definite answers. Realizing that for the first time in my life, my mother and I would have peace during the week, with no anxiety, no worry, I fell asleep with a smile. Now maybe I wouldn't have to tell Dottie about my secret life. I didn't have time to think about my one true love who walked me home that night.

The morning sunlight streamed through my open window. Little house sparrows chirped and twittered in the trees, waking me from a deep slumber. Sometime in the night, Mama had come in and raised my window to let a summer breeze dance in my room. It felt wonderful. I just laid there for a few minutes, then threw the cool sheet off of me, and sat on the side of the bed. I heard the radio playing in the kitchen. After putting my glasses on and seeing it was nearly eight o'clock, I rushed to the kitchen to see what my day was to bring.

She was dressed and drinking her coffee. "I was just getting ready to get you up."

"Where's Daddy?" I asked.

"He left early," she replied.

"When is he going to Lexington?" I asked in a low tone.

"I don't know," she said.

"What is wrong, Mama? Isn't this a good thing . . . him leaving?" I asked in frustration.

"What am I going to tell people?" Mama blurted, seemingly embarrassed.

For the first time, I let loose of some of the anger I stored in the dark places of my mind. "Oh God, Mama! What difference does it make? I don't care what people think, or what the neighbors think, or what anybody thinks! I don't care if the whole world knows."

Not only did my outburst frighten my mother, it scared me too. I didn't know where all that rage came from. I put my arms around my poor mother as she cried, ashamed that I had yelled at her. "Mama, I'm sorry. Please don't be mad at me. I didn't mean to make you cry."

"It's okay. Don't worry about it," she said as she pulled away from me. "I've got to go to work. I'm going to be late. Hurry up and get dressed."

In less than ten minutes, I was dressed and we were out the door, headed for Granny's. We didn't speak during the ride. When she dropped me off at Granny's house, she didn't even come in like she usually did. I felt sort of betrayed that she didn't seem happy. The morning went by quickly. Using the push mower, Granny mowed the yard with a fierce determination.

Drenched in sweat by 10 o'clock, Granny took a break to enjoy a cold drink of water. As she sat at the kitchen table, I wanted to tell her the news but I didn't know how.

"Susan, I have to get the grass cut before this afternoon because it's supposed to rain. And if it does, it'll take another day to dry up before I can get back out there with that mower. So you'll have to entertain yourself today. Besides, your mother only works til noon today," Granny said, wiping her brow with a rag.

"That's okay. I'm going to watch television anyway," I said, looking at the clock radio on the counter. "It's just two more hours. Granny, why don't you let me push the mower? I can do it."

"No, you might get hurt," she said. "It won't take as long as it has been. Then we'll have some lunch."

Granny was right. By noon the clouds gathered and she was back in the kitchen fixing us a grilled cheese sandwich, garnished with her homemade pickles on the side. To my surprise, even Mama sat down to enjoy a lunch with us instead of rushing home. *I'm enjoying this a little too much,* I thought.

As Mama drove us home, she began, "Honey, I'm sorry about this morning. Let's just see what happens, okay? I won't believe it until he actually leaves."

I nodded. There was nothing I could say to make my mother feel better. I had tried for years to find the good in whatever situation we fell into and I was running out of excuses. My fears of high school, my fears of being accepted, my fears of life in general were weighing me down.

At home, I called Dottie, asking her to meet me at the Rio Vista Bridge since that was about half way between us. Of course,

I got there before she did, simply because she was always late . . . for everything. This time I didn't mind. The concrete walkway attached to the bridge was a meeting place for boys with their bikes, men fishing for huge carp, and friends just getting together. I leaned against the low concrete wall, looking out on the clear waters of the Cumberland River. I finally decided I was going to have to tell Dottie. I had wrestled with an explanation about Friday night and couldn't come up with anything believable. I was going to tell her the truth. If she didn't want to have anything to do with me after that, I wouldn't blame her.

Dottie snuck up on me as I delved deep into thoughts and words. She poked me on the shoulder and then put her hands on her hips. "Okay, here I am," she said. "I want to know what is wrong with you? Why in the world did you ruin it? Sometimes, you act like you don't want to have anything to do with me."

I turned around to bravely face my best friend. "All right, I'm going to tell you something and you've got to swear on your life that you'll never tell a living soul, ever, and I really mean it."

"Good grief, okay, what is it?" Dottie whined.

"I don't know how to tell you this and it would take all day to tell you everything but here goes. The reason I don't ask you to spend the night much or ask you to come to the house a lot is because of Daddy. He drinks all the time and he is really mean. I wished I could have told you earlier but Mama made me promise not to tell anyone. Honestly, I shouldn't have even said anything now. Please don't say anything to my mother, okay?" I explained. "Daddy beats up on Mama nearly every night. Now you know why I tend to fall asleep in school. It's always been like this, as far back as I can remember."

There was a silence, as if time had stopped, and I wished so badly that I had lied to her instead. Maybe she thought I was lying anyway. Dottie stood with a stone face, showing no emotion, almost frightening."Why didn't you tell me this before? I thought I was your best friend."

I looked away from her. "I was afraid you would leave me, that you wouldn't want to have anything to do with me. My home isn't like your home. My house is full of nightmares," I said softly.

Then, surprisingly, Dottie put her arm around my shoulder and kissed my cheek. "Look, we are friends forever. Besides, you'll forget me anyway when you start high school. You're going to be going to the fancy city school and won't have time for me any more." She seemed so wise.

"Don't talk like that," I cried. "I can hardly stand this."

"I can't either," Dottie said. "Let's walk up to the Loyall Corner Store and get a cherry Coke."

Nothing was ever said again about my secret. At the time, I couldn't decide if Dottie chose to ignore it, thinking it would go away, or she had worse secrets that she couldn't talk about. Sometimes, serious things just seemed to go right over her head and I believe that was how she coped with life.

As we sat in a booth at the Corner Store sipping our drinks, my one true love came in with his friends. They played the pinball machine, played a record on the jukebox, and then left, not even looking our way. My heart pounded so loudly in my head that I couldn't hear Dottie's rambling nonsense. I couldn't breathe fast enough to calm myself down. I loved him so much. Dottie wanted to follow them but I looked out the window and saw them standing near the red light, hitchhiking.

Later that evening, Dottie and I made our regular night at the Youth Center. Once again, it was filled with the beautiful people, certainly not us. We just didn't fit in. Dottie was able to talk to other girls but I just stood there like a knot on a log. Unfortunately, my love didn't show up for me to admire that night. Dottie and I left the center a little early, feeling disappointed. This time she didn't ask to come in my house. I walked with her to the bridge, and nearly ran all the way back home. It was kinda creepy being alone in the dark. The streetlights brought shadows against the houses with my imagination leading me to wonder what was lurking behind the trees or under the bushes.

Within a few minutes I stood once again on my darkened porch. I took a deep breath and went inside, quickly shutting the door to keep the screaming from escaping outside. Little did I know that the noise was readily heard by those who walked close by.

Seeing Daddy bound through the house, stomping his feet, waving his arms, I got out of his way. "What's wrong?" I hollered, as I made it to the kitchen.

"He got a tooth pulled today and he's got a dry socket. He's been wailing ever since he got home. I told him to call the dentist but he won't. He thinks bourbon is going to cure it. Well, it's been three hours and it's not cured yet," Mama explained, frantically.

I peeped in living room to see him doubled over, roaring like a lion, screaming like a banshee. I didn't know if he was going to just fall face first over or just sit down and pass out. Then he raised back up and rushed back in the kitchen, grabbing his bottle and guzzling a long drink. His black hair fell in wild mess from where he had been pulling it, trying to stop the pain. His swollen bloodshot eyes revealed a sort of helplessness. He reeked of a putrid odor. Mama ran hot water in a washcloth and gave it to him to put on his jaw. It didn't help. *At least, he's not able to hit her,* I thought. I felt no compassion. I wished he'd just shut up. That scared me. *How could I be so mean?*

Around three a.m., Daddy was so exhausted with pain and out of bourbon that he finally passed out in his chair. Mama and I went to bed. In just a few hours we had to go to Mass.

Mama shook my shoulder, calling my name until I rolled over and opened my eyes. "Come on, Susan, it's time to get up," she said, sweetly. "Get ready for church."

I must have slept like the dead because my bedding, even my pillow, didn't look like I laid there. Wearing my yellow dress with a white eyelet overlay, I whirled around in front of my mirror to make sure my slip wasn't showing. I looked slimmer wearing my garter belt to hold my nylons and my one-inch heels. After several attempts to fix my hair, I relented and wadded most of the strands under my white pillbox hat. Mama just rolled her eyes at my new look. I thought I looked sophisticated.

"Mama, isn't Daddy getting up?" I asked.

"No, let him sleep. Come on, let's go. I'm afraid we're going to be late," she said.

As we drove through Harlan, over Bailey Hill and past Jack's Drive-In, my thoughts took me to a different place, a place of happiness and peace, only focused in my mind, knowing the possibility was fruitless. "Mama, when is Daddy leaving?"

"He said he was leaving on the bus this afternoon. But I don't know if that was the whiskey talking or him.

At church, Mama and I sat in our familiar pew, in the third row from the back, next to the aisle. Many of the original parishioners seemed to claim a seat in chosen pews. It was just understood. Large families took up the whole pew and usually sat in the back pews due to crying babies and fussy toddlers. A few times Dottie would sit with me but that stopped when we couldn't resist whispering during the priest's homily.

By the time, Mass was over and we were back in the car, I was hungry. "Mama, are we stopping at Granny's? I'm starved to death.

"No, honey, we need to get on home. If your Daddy is really leaving, then I need to pack his clothes," she answered. "And if he isn't leaving, we need to get home anyway."

I knew as soon as Mama opened the front door that something was bad. Daddy was sitting in his chair in the living room, slumped to the side. We stood there, staring at him, myself wondering if he was dead. After an eternity of seconds, I spoke, "Daddy, wake up. Are you asleep? Hey, wake up!" I knew not to touch him as the last time I shook his shoulder while he was asleep, he raised up with his fist drawn back to hit me. Only my scream had stopped him then.

Daddy mumbled, drool sliding down his cheek. He batted his eyes. In a flash, he jumped up, grabbed the car keys out of Mama's hand and left, slamming the front door so hard it rattled the pictures on the wall.

"Well, I don't suppose he is leaving today. Come on, Susan, I'll fix us something to eat," Mama said. "He's probably going to the bootlegger."

Mama was right. Daddy returned after a couple of hours carrying his brown paper sack. Strangely, he looked better. He said he found the dentist walking out of the Baptist Church in town, stopped and told him about the pain. The dentist met him at the office and packed the hole with medicine and gauze.

"He gave me these pain pills but I ain't taking them," Daddy said, holding out his hand, then dropping the pills down the kitchen sink. "Bourbon will do just fine."

He sat at the kitchen table with the open half pint while Mama heated up leftovers from our Sunday dinner. She hoped that a meal would slow down the effects of the alcohol and he may not become a crazed drunk. On the other hand, if his chewing irritated his sore gums, it could cause more pain . . . for all of us.

While Daddy ate, Mama and I went to Resthaven to visit Granddaddy's grave. We were only gone about half an hour but in those minutes, Daddy emerged as a raving lunatic when we got home. It was early afternoon, a hot muggy day with all our windows and doors closed.

"Mama, please let's leave. Let's go to Granny's or just drive around," I begged.

"You know I can't leave. Here's fifty cents," she said, handing me the coins. "You sneak out and go to the movies. Stay as long as you want."

"He's sitting where he can see the front door and the back door. How am I going to get out?" I asked in a whisper.

"I don't know. Maybe I can distract him," she answered.

While Mama sat in the living room with Daddy, I tried to get out the front door but he had locked it and kept the key. I was sure that Mama didn't know. It was impossible to get out the back door without him seeing me. I went in the bathroom and shut the door trying to figure out a way to leave. *The answer is right in front of me. I'll climb out the bathroom window*, I thought. And that is what I did. I balanced myself on the edges of the bathtub, opened the window, and pulled myself through. It was a short drop to the ground. I ran through the back alley and onto the street where I stopped to check my clothes. *I did it!*

The guilt set in and I began to worry about what he would do when he found out I was gone. Would he take it out on Mama and did I make things worse? It was too late. I went to the movies and sat in a dark corner alone. I was distracted by lovers kissing shamelessly in the front row. When the movie was over, the lights came on. I was devastated, crushed, hurt beyond words. The boy that took my breath away had his arm around a girl, whispering something in her ear. I ran out of the theater and started home. Then I realized, *What am I doing? Why am I going home? Can I go home now? Maybe Daddy is asleep.*

My head ached as I approached my house. I turned the door knob to enter but it was still locked. I knocked on the door. No one came. I knocked again and then beat loudly on the wooden door. I knocked on the window, rattling the pane. Nothing. I became scared, thinking the worst. I sat down on the edge of the porch for less than a minute and then knocked again. "Hey, let me in!" I shouted, pounding fiercely.

Suddenly, the door opened. Daddy stared at me, turned and walked into the bedroom, saying nothing. I started through the house, looking for Mama or maybe a dead body. I found her laying in the bed, her eyes glassy and strange. She looked at me but said nothing. I didn't want to know.

I sat in the living room alone, watching television, unsure of what I was supposed to do. Finally, Mama joined me on the couch.

"Did you have a good time at the movies?" she asked, reaching up and stroking my hair.

I nodded. Feeling very uneasy I said, "I'm going to bed."

"But, honey, it's still early," Mama answered.

"I know," I said, "But I'm tired."

As I curled up in my bed, I squeezed my eyes as tightly as I could. *Maybe when I open my eyes, all of this will be gone*, I prayed. I wiped beads of sweat off of my forehead. *When is he going to leave?* Nighttime finally settled in my room. It was easier to hide in the darkness.

CHAPTER EIGHT

When the first week of high school began after Labor Day, the halls of Harlan High were overrun with students finding their assigned home rooms, classes, and lockers. The freshly waxed hardwood floors and the strong smell of polish gave the sense of newness to the old two story brick building. Lost in the hallways and unfamiliar classroom doors, I became the little mouse in a lab maze. Feeling smothered, overwhelmed, and helpless, my hands dripped in sweat as I carried my papers and books to my home room. I wanted so badly to run out of the school, but instead I tried to blend in . . . into the walls. I knew immediately I didn't fit in. The requirements for being accepted at the city school were far above my reach. My family had no money and no clout. I was not pretty and only knew a few of the former Holy Trinity students that went to Harlan High. I didn't know how to be social, to make friends, to be sought after. *If Dottie was with me, I could bear this*, I thought. *I feel so alone.*

Dottie and I began to go our separate ways. It wasn't our preference. It was just the natural process of growing up. I hated it. At first we called each other every day but then as time went by, the distance grew too great.

In an effort to be liked, I went to all the ball games, joined a of couple clubs, and attempted to sit near the popular kids. The few friendships I did make were only during school hours.

Weeks went by. I had given up on Daddy's plan to leave. My first report card brought shame in my efforts to be smart. As I stared at the D– in Algebra, the A's and B's in the other subjects paled. After school, I walked down to Mama's office with dread. I had failed her once again. I watched as her expression change.

"Well, what are you going to do about this? You can't get on the honor roll with a grade like this," Mama said.

I looked down at the floor. "I don't know. I really tried."

"Here, take this and go show your Daddy," she ordered, handing me the card back. "I'm really disappointed in you, young lady."

"But, Mama . . . " I started.

"Go on. He's at the barber shop," she said. "Go on before it closes."

I took the card and left, not understanding the meaning of her actions. Terrified, I walked slowly to the shop, jaywalking across the street. *Maybe I'll get hit by a truck and not have to do this*, I thought. The light inside the shop showed no customers. I was glad of that. Daddy was sitting in his barber chair. The other barbers had already left for the day. He looked so sad, so lonely.

"Hi, Daddy," I said as I stepped inside the open doorway.

He looked up, surprised and seemingly sober. "Well, Susan, what are you doing here?"

"Daddy, I got my report card today and Mama said I had to show it to you," I rambled. "I did really good on everything but math. I didn't make the honor roll."

With tears, I handed him the shameful report card. Not saying a word, he stared at the results for what it seemed as an eternity. Then he looked up at me and smiled.

"Come over here," he said softly, reaching his arm out to me.

A little apprehensive of his intentions, I slowly let him put his arm around me. A tear fell on my blouse. I didn't know if it was the end of me or the end of the world.

"Did you do the best you could?" he asked.

"Oh, yes, Daddy, I did. I stayed after school so the teacher could tutor me some. Even the teacher finally decided I couldn't understand it. You can ask him yourself. I really tried," I pleaded.

"Don't worry about it," Daddy whispered. "You can't be good in everything. Just look at the other grades. You'll be okay. Just keep trying."

For the first time, I looked at my Daddy in a different way. Maybe he did understand. Maybe deep down he wasn't the evil person I saw at nighttime. Maybe there was two of him.

As Mama and I went home that afternoon, the roar of the car engine and the noise of the tires on the pavement kept the quiet from invading the air. After she parked the car in front of the house, she turned to me.

"Well, what did your Daddy say?"

"Nothing," I answered, not wanting to tell her what really happened.

"Well, that figures," she quipped and got out of the car.

The next few nights were tolerable and I didn't dare question Mama, Daddy, or God. Because the tension ran high when all of us were in the same room, Mama usually sat in the kitchen, Daddy in the living room, and I kept to myself in my bedroom. I pondered Daddy's kindness to me so much that I began to believe he had changed. Wrong again.

On a Friday night, he staggered home soon after dark. Tripping over a foot stool he hit his head on the wall. Enraged, shouting that Mama had put the stool in his way, he doubled his fist up and rammed it into the wall.

Mama jumped out of bed and ran into the living room. "What in God's name are you doing?" she asked.

Wailing, Daddy stood there holding his bloody hand. "What are you trying to do, kill me?"

"You're crazy. Come in here before you get blood all over the rug," she said, going into the kitchen.

I watched in the darkness of my room while Mama wrapped Daddy's hand at the kitchen table.

"Where in the hell did that stool come from?" he asked.

"It's always been there. It's never been moved," she answered. "You're drunk."

"Shut up!" Daddy yelled. "Just shut up!"

She didn't shut up. "I thought you were going to go to Lexington. You had all these big ideas."

With those words, I knew it was going to turn bad. Daddy raised up from the table, kicked the chair back with his foot, leaned over and slapped Mama on the side of her head with his left hand, making a sharp piercing sound. Mama screamed and grabbed her ear. I jumped up and ran into the kitchen. Somehow I pushed Daddy back down in the chair.

"Mama! Are you all right?" I cried. "Mama!"

I turned to Daddy. "Daddy, go to bed!"

So surprised by my fury, he smiled, got up, and went into the bedroom.

Mama cried for a long time, the excruciating pain subsiding by daylight. I cleaned a trickle of blood that oozed out of her ear. I tried to hold her as she sat on the couch because laying down made the pain worse. By morning, we were exhausted.

"Susan, I can't hear out of this side," Mama said, holding a warm damp washcloth over her ear. "I think he burst my eardrum."

"Please go to the doctor. I'll go with you," I begged.

"No, I can't. Besides most of the doctors are his drinking buddies. It's too embarrassing," she explained. "And they might say something."

I was ready to stand at the top of Pine Mountain and shout to the world what was going on in my family. Mama refused to leave, Daddy wanted all of us to leave, and I was tired of praying for something that never was going to happen.

During lunchtime at school, most of the kids walked about three blocks downtown to eat. I usually walked by myself, stopping in front of Mama's office next door to Creech Drug Store first, just to wave at her. Although there were several cafes in town, and the four drug stores, Creech's was always crowded during the lunch hour with regular patrons and school kids. Lately, I was lucky enough to get a seat in a booth with some of the students in my classes. I found that if I just listened to them, nodded and agreed, I didn't get scared and choke on my food. On the Monday following Daddy's rampage, I sat in Creech Drug at lunchtime with a group of three classmates, two boys and one girl. It wasn't like I was invited to sit with them. I had asked and since I was holding an order of fries and a coke, they said okay. Of course, as soon as I sat down, they helped themselves to my food.

"Hey, Susan, I hitched a ride Friday night to come and see you," the dark-haired boy from Ivy Hill said. "But when I walked on your porch, I heard your Daddy screaming and cussing so I took off."

Everyone laughed but me. I just sat there wishing I were dead. I had no excuse to give them. I got up and ran out of the drug store, even forgetting to pay for my lunch. I ran into Mama's office, tearing streaming.

"What's wrong, honey?" Mama asked, hanging up the phone and putting her arms around me. "What happened?"

After telling her the story, she looked at me sternly. "It's not your fault. That boy ought to be ashamed of himself. Don't pay any attention to him."

"But, Mama, how am I going to go back to school after this?" I sobbed.

"You will go back because you have to. It'll get better," she said, soothingly. "Now go on before the bell rings. I have to get back to work."

I dried my eyes and went back to school, sure that the halls were filled with laughter directed at me. By the time my class began, I felt exhausted and sleepy. The room was warm and soon my eyelids closed. The teacher, I later learned was one of my mother's friends, so she didn't embarrass me. Although I dozed less than five minutes, it startled me when I suddenly awoke as she was writing on the blackboard. I knew that she had caught me. Since I figured she would send me to the principal's office for sleeping anyway, I was just going to tell her what was going on in my life and beg for help. I really needed someone. When the bell rang and everyone had left the room, she asked me to come up to her desk.

"I'm sorry for sleeping in class. I just couldn't help it," I explained. "I know I'm not doing too good in this class but I'll try harder. I just have a hard time at home, with my daddy and everything."

There, I said it. I gave her an opening. I waited for her to reach out, to ask me what was the problem, to offer to help me. It didn't happen. She looked at me with such pitiful eyes and said, "Susan, I know you are doing your best. I'm sorry."

"I need . . . ," I began.

"Susan, you need to get to your last class or you will be tardy," the teacher interrupted.

For a second, I stood there dumbfounded, clutching my books to my chest, wondering if it was really happening. I nodded and left, walking through the hallway like a robot. *No one was going to help me. No one. This is how it's going to be. No one wants to get involved. It is my problem,* I realized. *Mama doesn't want any help, Daddy doesn't think he needs help, and I can't find help.*

A few days after the drug store fiasco, I discovered that Daddy really was going to move to Lexington. I didn't know if Mama told Daddy about the boy from Ivy Hill or if my teacher said something to Mama. It didn't matter. Joyfully, Mama and I packed his bags and drove him to the Greyhound Bus Station. Daddy and I played the pinball machine while Mama sat on one of the benches. We sat in the photo booth and had our pictures taken together, a strip of four photos, with smiling faces. He hugged me and kissed my forehead, telling that he would be back the following weekend. Mama and I stood while he got on the bus and took a seat. I waved to him as he looked out the tinted window. When the bus pulled out, I knew God had answered a prayer. *Thank you, God.*

For the first time, Mama and I had a whole week to ourselves. We ate at Granny's most afternoons. Mama gave Granny an elaborate excuse for Daddy going to Lexington to work. Granny seemed to agree that there was money to be made in the big cities, that it was a good opportunity for him. She never mentioned that Mama shouldn't leave Harlan but it was set in stone anyway. And I didn't have any desire to go anywhere now.

Although I still dreaded weekends, it was a trade off for a week of peace. Daddy rode the bus overnight on Fridays, arriving in Harlan by daylight. He ate breakfast at one of the local cafes and then caught a ride to the local bootleggers. By early afternoon, he usually called Mama, ranting and raving. Then late Saturday nights, he would finally come home, ready to raise hell. As November approached, so did the cold weather. It was getting increasing difficult for us to run outside and hide behind the coal bin or the maple tree in the backyard, especially if we were barefooted.

Late that fall, on November 22, 1963, I watched a boy run through the school halls, flailing his skinny arms and screaming, "They've killed him! President Kennedy is dead!" I felt numb, unable to comprehend the impact. The halls quietly filled with a mass of students, not even a whisper echoed in the building. We were sick with fear as we settled into our classrooms. Teachers comforted the students. The principal spoke on the intercom. Someone said aloud, "Our country doesn't have a president. We don't have a leader."

After school I ran down to Mama's office, passing adults crying in the streets. Mama was crying at her desk. I wanted to cry, but I couldn't. We watched Walter Cronkite cry on television. Two days later, we were shocked further as television captured Jack Ruby coming out of nowhere and shooting Lee Harvey Oswald. Mama cried, Daddy cried. It seemed the whole world was crying. The news reporters echoed, "The first Catholic President of the United States of America, dead."

Thanksgiving that year in the midst of the nation's mourning kept families busy. We went to Granny's as usual, enjoying the relatives and good food, giving thanks for all our blessings. Daddy didn't make it in from Lexington because of a wonderfully unexpected early snowfall. He called, giving the excuse that the roads were too bad and that he had to work on Friday anyway. Mama and I didn't care. Then, feeling selfish, I prayed that he wouldn't come in over the holiday weekend. Still, he showed up, drunk, without a suitcase. Apparently, he had hidden a bottle in his coat pocket, sat in the back of the Greyhound, and drank nearly all night. He went straight to bed, and slept all day. Mama and I left, picked up Granny, and went to the grocery. We didn't mention that Daddy was home.

Mama fixed Thanksgiving leftovers: turkey, dressing and all the trimmings for supper. Daddy ate heartily and seemed to be in a jovial mood.

"By the way, I'm going to catch the bus back to Lexington tonight," Daddy said. "I've got a chance to make me some big money."

"What do you mean, big money?" she asked. "What are you getting into?"

"Never you mind. I know what I'm doing," he answered. "Just shut up!"

This time Mama hushed.

"By the way, you don't have to take me to the bus station. I'm hitching a ride," he said.

After he finished his meal, he got up to leave. "Susan, I love you. You're all I've got in this world."

I looked up at him, seeing a glimpse of a human being. "Daddy, I love you too."

Daddy started to say something to Mama but quickly decided not to. Mama didn't look up from her plate of untouched food.

When Daddy left, Mama spoke up. "Honey, don't kid yourself. If he gets any money at all, we'll never see it. So please don't expect anything. I learned that a long time ago."

She was right. We never knew when he was lying. He continued to return on the weekends, sometimes in a rage, occasionally with a calmer facade. The only thing we knew for sure was that he would leave on Sunday and for that I was thankful.

My social life improved, a little. Occasionally, in the mornings before the first bell, I sat in the gym with a couple of girls who seemed to know about every rock-n-roll singer whoever lived and died. I learned a lot from them, just by listening. One conversation had already begun when I walked up to them.

"You know, they're coming over here. I think they will arrive in February," the petite freckle-faced girl said. "Oh, I would die to see them."

"What's coming?" I asked.

"The Beatles!" she announced as if I was the dumbest person alive. "It's an invasion!"

For a second, I thought it was it was a swarm of bugs attacking the United States. I had never heard of the Beatles. Then I realized it was about music.

"Susan, do you live under a rock? Look at all those magazines at Creech Drug. Their pictures are on nearly all of them. There's four of them," the tall dark haired girl said. "They are going to be on the Ed Sullivan Show too."

I made a mental note to check out those magazines. "Oh, yeah, that's right. That Ed Sullivan Show has some pretty good acts. I just love that mouse, Topo Gigio," I answered. "I got to watch Elvis on there a few years ago. Of course, it only showed the top half of him."

The two girls looked at each other, then at me, and rolled their eyes. Luckily, the bell rang.

The weeks went by too fast and Christmas arrived with all the festivities. The town's store windows were dressed in red, green, and gold. The Harlan County courthouse decorated the front lawn with the lighted manger scene as well as multicolored lights on tall Christmas pines. Businesses flourished. That Christmas I was going to fulfill my promise, to myself, one that I made years earlier.

Instead of eating lunch every day at school, I would just buy a coke and save the rest of my change. I didn't tell Mama although she mentioned a few times about me raiding the refrigerator before supper. Instead of buying my favorite chocolate covered raisins at the movies, I put the money in my shoe and added it to my savings stashed away in an old bobbie sock hidden underneath my thick red Webster Dictionary in my bottom desk drawer.

By the time school was out for Christmas break, I had saved nearly fifteen dollars. On the evening of the Christmas parade, all the stores in Harlan stayed open late for shoppers. The streets lined with children, anxious to see Santa Claus on the big red fire truck. The marching bands from each school played carols as the decorated floats moved slowly through the streets. Mama and I stood on the corner of Central and Second Street, right in front of her office. Although I was a teenager, I soon got caught up in the joy of being a kid, and found myself waving to Santa. Mama seemed to enjoy the moment also.

As the end of the parade inched down toward Main Street, I told Mama that I was going to run on down to the dime store and get some cashews.

"Do you want me to go with you?" she asked.

"No, that's okay. Mama, I'm in high school. I can take care of myself just fine. Why don't you wait on me in Creech Drug? I'll only be a few minutes," I suggested. "Besides, it's really getting cold!"

"Okay, but don't take too long. The fire will be out in the furnace and it'll take forever to get the house warm," she said.

I did go to Scott's Five and Dime, in one door, bought a nickel's worth of nuts, and back out the door. Then I went to the Quality Shop, a fancy ladies' dress shop. I didn't know that the lady behind the counter knew my mother and my whole family. I walked over to a rack of dresses, hanging so neatly as if no one had ever touched them. I smiled at the woman. She smiled back, her ruby red lipstick stretching across her face.

"Can I help you, honey?" she asked kindly. "Are you buying for yourself or a present?"

I suddenly became embarrassed. "Oh, no, not for me. It's for my mother . . . Christmas you know," I stammered.

She motioned for me to come over to the other side of the store. "Why don't you pick out a few things right here and then you can decide?" she suggested, holding up a beautiful winter white suit with a white fur collar.

My eyes lit up. I ran my fingers over the fur and down the sleeves. "Oh, it's just beautiful," I exclaimed. "It's lined and everything."

"If it doesn't fit, you can bring it back. But I just bet it will fit your mother just fine," she said.

"How much is it?" I asked, terrified of her answer.

"Well, how much are you planning on spending?" she asked.

I raised my heavy shoulder purse and answered, "I have fifteen dollars and twenty cents." *Please God, let that be enough*, I prayed.

The lady pulled the twenty-five dollar price tag off the suit, showed it to me, then stuck it in her pocket. "You are so lucky!" she said. "We're having a Christmas sale tonight and this suit is retailing for fifteen dollars."

"I'll take it!" I exclaimed. "Can you wrap it up for me? I don't want Mama to see it."

The woman folded the suit neatly in a box and wrapped it with holiday paper and ribbons. She put Mama's present in a large bag and rang up the cash register. "That'll be fifteen dollars and twenty cents exactly. I have to charge for the wrapping paper and bows this year. Hope you don't mind."

I was so happy. I poured all the coins out on the counter and began counting.

She stared down all the pile of change and laughed. "I'll tell you what, if you say there's fifteen dollars and twenty cents in this mess, I'm going to believe you. When I count it later, if I come up short, I'll let you know."

"Oh, I promise it's all there," I said. "Thank you so very much.

As I opened the door to leave, I turned back to her and said, "Merry Christmas."

"Merry Christmas to you, honey. I know your mother will be happy," she answered.

Before I met up with Mama at Creech Drug, I hid her present in the floor of the backseat of the car which was parked near the Courthouse. In the darkness, she never noticed her present when she slid into the driver's seat to drive home and I didn't dare glance to the backseat. Sure enough, we did walk into a very cold house. While she was building a fire in the furnace, I ran back outside, got the bag, and hid it under my bed. *It's going to be a good Christmas*, I thought.

As usual, our tree was decorated with old and new balls, bulbs, and tinsel. We placed the little manger set under the tree along with my old *Twas The Night Before Christmas* book. Six presents to be exact laid around the tree, four for me and two for Daddy. A pine needle wreath with a red velvet bow hung on the front door, a first for our house. Mama and I enjoyed the festive decorating without worry, another first.

Early Christmas Eve, Daddy walked through the door as if he owned the world. "Ho, ho, ho! I'm home!" he exclaimed.

After putting his suitcase in the bedroom, he set a fancy department store paper bag on the kitchen table. He reached in and carefully laid down two gifts wrapped in shiny gold foil.

"Here's a present, for each of you. It cost me a pretty penny but nothing's too good for the women in my life," he boasted. "Only the best!"

Mama and I stood there, motionless. Finally, I spoke, "Daddy, what is it? Give me a hint!"

"No, you'll just have to wait until morning," he said. "Come here and give your old man a hug."

It was Christmas. My heart yearned for the love of family, just one time. I hugged my father. "Daddy, I'm glad you're home." I wanted so badly to mean it.

Mama didn't say a word. She stood at the kitchen sink, smoking her cigarette, evaluating what just took place in front of her eyes. She poured Daddy a cup of coffee and handed it to him with obvious caution.

The evening was strange, no fussing or fighting, no ranting or raving. Mama was on edge, waiting for the bomb to drop. Of course, Daddy had been drinking but it seemed he was making an effort to be nice. I was so leery of the change that I became lightheaded.

Driving us to midnight Mass, Daddy joked, whistled a tune, and became this stranger who was likeable. Mama talked when necessary, trying to keep the peace. In my nervousness, I jabbered, laughed at Daddy's jokes, all the while squeezing my hands together. *Dear God, please let this be a good Christmas. Please don't let Daddy raise hell, just this once, please,* I prayed.

The church service was beautiful as usual. I caught myself yawning several times, not from boredom but from finally being able to relax a little. After Mass, as Mama and I knelt in front of the manger once again, this time I knew what to say. *Jesus, I know I shouldn't be asking for something on Your birthday, but please help us have a good Christmas this year. Keep Mama safe and help Daddy fix his problems,* I prayed. *And God, thank You for making a way for me to buy Mama that present. Amen.*

Dottie and her family arrived late. Unfortunately, by the time I got outside after the service, they had already left. I missed my best friend so much.

When we got home, I mentally prepared myself for a night of terror. Instead, I got a surprise. I began to think aliens had kidnaped my father and this was a clone, only better. After changing out of his suit, Daddy fixed a hillbilly milkshake, crumbling cornbread in a glass and pouring milk over it and eating it with a spoon. Mama and I hung our dresses back up for one more wear and put on our pajamas and robes.

"Daddy, I'm sleepy. I'm going to go on to bed," I said and kissed his cheek. "I love you."

Daddy swallowed his bite of cornbread and put his arm around me. "I love you too. Merry Christmas."

Mama followed me into my bedroom. As I slid between the bedcovers, she leaned over and kissed my forehead. "Good night, Susan, I love you."

"Nite, Mama, I love you too," I said. "Merry Christmas."

Mama turned out my light. "Merry Christmas to you, honey," she answered.

Although no words were exchanged, our looks to each other were enough. Neither one of us was going to say anything for fear of breaking the Christmas spell. I soon fell asleep, not waking until morning. There had been no fighting, no screaming. It was still quiet in the house, no one was stirring. It was daylight. I panicked. *Oh God, did something happen and I slept through it?*

I jumped out of bed and hurried to the kitchen. Mama and Daddy were sitting at the table drinking coffee, quiet as a whisper. They turned to me and said, "Merry Christmas, Susan."

"Come on. Let's go into the living room so you can open your presents," Mama suggested.

I giggled, thinking I was in a dream. Mama and Daddy sat on the couch while I tore and tossed wrapping paper and bows. "Oh, thank you, thank you! I just love it!" I exclaimed, holding up a beautiful red sweater. A smaller box contained a silver charm bracelet and another box held a pair of boots I had wanted from Belk's. The fourth present was a black long sleeve A-line dress with a white frilly lace draped down the front. It was beautiful.

"Now, open your presents from me," Daddy said, handing Mama and me our presents.

She stared at hers for a second and then we opened our boxes together. Such a surprise! A bottle of Bluegrass Cologne for each of us, a very expensive gift from the big city. Mama's eyes widened. All she could say was, "Thank you." She sprayed some of hers on her wrist and I sprayed some on my neck. The rich scent danced in the air.

I grabbed the two presents tagged for Daddy. "Here, open them!"

Daddy held his new tie clasp and cuff links in his hand for me to see. His second gift brought a smile and a hint of a tear in his eyes. Mama had bought him a new fishing reel, a Zebco. He choked, "Thank you so much. It's perfect."

"Oh, wait a minute. I almost forgot," I shouted as I rushed to get Mama's present from under my bed. "Here, Mama."

With a frown on her face, she opened the box, folded the white tissue back to reveal the white suit. Gently she ran her fingers over the fur collar. She sobbed. It scared me. Daddy laughed.

"What'd I do wrong, Mama?" I asked. "If you don't like it, you can take it back. The woman at the shop said so."

"No, it's beautiful. I love it. It's just such a surprise. How in the world did you pay for it?" Mama asked. "When did you get it?"

"I saved my lunch money forever. I bought it the night of the parade and hid it in the car. Then I stuck it under my bed," I explained.

A touch of Christmas magic shone on our faces that day. Realizing it may never happen again, I cherished every minute.

CHAPTER NINE

For two years, I chose to emotionally withdraw, feeding my insecurities. However, after passing my driver's test, I found an amazing independence. Mama's old black Studebaker certainly didn't give me any status with my peers. However, it didn't matter to me any longer that I didn't fit in with the rich city kids. My license provided me with a glorious amount of freedom and the opportunity to make friends. Unfortunately, I couldn't risk inviting anyone to my house. Daddy had moved back home.

I always knew there was a threat of his return but as the months passed, I had become more comfortable with his absence during the week. The weekends became a punishment for the peaceful weekdays. However, in the spring of 1966, Daddy decided to move back home. He got a job at a different barber shop in town and seemed to be well accepted. He was a master of deception with his customers, a sharp contrast from the evil drunk at home.

I spent my summer nights either in the dark at the Margie Grand Theater or trying to blend in at the local bowling alley. One Friday night in the very noisy and crowded bowling alley, I met a boy. His dark hair, kind face, and warm smile attracted me. Larry seemed older than the year difference between out ages. I found out that night our birthdays were on the same day. I thought our meeting was meant to be. He called me as soon as

I got home, continuing to call me several times a day. It was easy in the beginning to keep it a secret from Mama as she rarely talked to me about personal things. Yet, somehow she found out that I was meeting a boy at the movies, going to the drive-in, and sneaking him into the house when no one was home.

"I do not want you to see that boy," Mama ordered, visibly upset. "He's bad news."

"Okay," I agreed, absolutely determined to see him again.

With the forbidden fruit dangling in front of me, I was positive that I was in love and no one, even my mother, was going to keep me from him. I just became more careful when sneaking around with him. After feeling so lonely for so long, I had found someone and I wasn't about to give him up, for anyone.

On a Saturday afternoon in late July, Daddy went fishing with one of his drinking buddies, returning unexpectedly early Sunday morning. He went to bed as Mama and I left for church. I lit a candle in front of the statue of the Virgin Mary after Mass, praying for a reprieve. I resented my mother trying to hold onto me. The harder she clung, the more I tried to pull away. I felt she should have saved me from this unstable life. I concealed my contempt for my father who led two lives. He had a likable, jovial personality with his friends and the dark side he showed only to his family. I was full of conflicting emotions.

Driving home from Mass, Mama gave me an opportunity to speak my mind with one sentence. "You know, Susan, all I want for you is the best."

"Mama, why don't you leave Daddy?" I asked. "I mean, we could get an apartment in town, or live with Granny, or leave and start somewhere else all brand new."

"I can't leave. I've told you that before," she said, gripping the steering wheel with both hands.

My frustration built. "I just don't see why!" I said loudly. "God would understand. I can't believe that He wants you to live like this!"

"I don't want to burden Granny by living with her. I have a job here so we can't leave Harlan," she explained. "It's just too much . . . "

"Well, then why can't we just get an apartment in town or just anywhere?" I pleaded.

"If we left, I'm afraid he'd kill me," Mama confessed.

"Was he always like this?" I asked. "I mean, I can't remember him being any other way."

"He always drank but he got worse after you were born," she explained. "I don't know what happened. Maybe I gave you too much attention or something. What difference does it make?"

Shocked by my mother's words, I didn't know if she was blaming me or herself.

"Mama, if we don't get out, I'm afraid I'm going to find you dead anyway," I cried. "Please just think about it. We can make it. You pay all the bills anyway. I won't ask for a thing."

For the rest of the ride, we were silent. When we got home, it was a different story. Daddy was waiting in the kitchen. I went directly into my room.

He grabbed Mama by the nape of her neck and pushed her against the refrigerator. "Fix me something to eat!" he demanded.

Mama pulled away. "Can't you just wait until I change clothes?" she begged. "We just got out of church. Please don't do this on Sunday."

Daddy retreated to the living room. "Hurry up!"

I quickly changed clothes. Thinking that if I kept Daddy occupied, then it wouldn't be so bad for Mama. I joined Daddy watching television until she called us for dinner.

The meal was pleasant enough, especially since Daddy apparently was starved. Mama's pork chops and mashed potatoes were a favorite of Daddy's even though he never acknowledged it to her. It felt awkward, watching Mama play with her food while Daddy stuffed his mouth. I wasn't hungry.

Usually I met Larry at the movies on Sunday but he was in Ohio visiting his family. I had a feeling that the day would be long and painful. I was right. As soon as we finished a slice of homemade cherry pie for dessert, Daddy took his empty glass and threw it against the wall, shattering slivers of glass on the table and wall. He stood up, kicked his chair backward tipping it over, and returned to the living room. I helped Mama pick up the broken glass up and clean the kitchen.

"Come in here! Turn the television channels for me," he ordered. "There's got to be a western on somewhere."

Mama obeyed. "I'm sorry but there's not any cowboys on right now," she apologized while turning the knob. "Maybe later."

"Daddy, why don't you take a nap and when you wake up, maybe we can find one then?" I suggested.

"I'm not sleepy. Go get me my half pint under the kitchen sink, Susan. I'll just sit right here," he responded. "I don't need a glass."

After a couple of huge gulps from the bottle, Daddy closed his eyes. Soon I heard snoring. Not knowing if he passed out or was asleep, it really didn't make any difference. I tiptoed into the kitchen to see Mama staring once again out the window. I wondered if she wished as I did, that she could just fly away, disappear into thin air, as if she never existed.

"Mama, I'm going to go riding," I whispered. "Maybe, go up to Mike's Drive-In for a while."

"You're not going to meet that boy, are you?" she asked.

I shook my head. I was telling her the truth although I would have lied in a heartbeat to be with him. I drove past Granny's house, wanting to stop and visit but then more lies would have been told. At Baxter, I drove over the old road next to the railroad tracks, returning to Loyall. Still not wanting to go home, I went to the cemetery and parked. I got out of the car, walked up the hillside, and sat beside Granddaddy's plot, overlooking hundreds of grave markers. The hot afternoon sun cast shadows under the trees giving the illusion of coolness. A few visitors carried flowers to various tombstones, honoring their dead. Granddaddy's marker had a beautiful red and white floral arrangement. It was important to Mama and Granny although I could not see that Granddaddy would care one way or the other.

"Granddaddy, I just can't go on like this," I said aloud. "I don't know what to do. She won't leave but I think anything would be better than this. Sometimes, I think I'll run away but then what would Mama do."

I sat on the ground, pulling up tiny blades of grass and swatting sweat bees for nearly an hour. As much as I dreaded it, I had to go home.

When I walked into my house, I knew I should have come home sooner. I found Mama leaning over the bathroom sink holding a wet washcloth to her bloody nose.

"Where's Daddy?" I asked, glancing behind me.

"He left a few minutes ago," she mumbled.

"Mama, please let's leave. Please!" I cried.

"Susan, you're being ridiculous," Mama fussed. "Hush, and go get me some ice in a clean washcloth."

As darkness covered the little house on Bailey Street, my mother and I sat motionless together on the couch pretending to watch television. Each in our own thoughts, we dared not mention what the night would bring. We didn't have to wait long. Daddy entered the front door, slamming it back against the wall. He ran through the house and opened the back door, all without saying a word. This was behavior we hadn't seen before but knew enough to be fearful. Mama grabbed my hand and we ran out the front door. We sat in the car for a long time. The keys were next to Mama's pocketbook on the coffee table. It didn't matter. There was no place to go. I fell asleep twice, each time waking up with a jerk. Mama kept watch. As daylight broke, we ventured back into the house. Daddy was asleep. The odor made me want to vomit. Mama opened the windows, letting fresh clean air in to cover the stench of whiskey and cigarettes. She dressed for work, using heavy pancake makeup to cover her bruises. At a quick glance, she looked just fine. Her nose, still a bit swollen, was not broken. Or as least, she decided it wasn't. I didn't bother telling her to go to the doctor. She didn't go when Daddy burst her ear drum so why would she go now?

"Here, you take me to work and you can use the car today," she said, handing me the keys. "You don't need to stay home right now. Your Daddy will go to work later and you can come home then."

"Where do you want me to go?" I asked. "Can I go to Granny's?"

"Nooo, don't go to Granny's. She's got enough to deal with besides wondering why you are up there so early," she answered. "Just find somewhere to go."

So I drove Mama to work, trying to figure out where to go. Then suddenly I became infuriated, angry that I had no where to go and no one to go to. I stopped at a pay phone, gathered all my coins, and called Larry, the only person in the world who cared. Before I realized it, I blurted out nearly my whole life story, not knowing whether he believed me and not really caring.

"Look, if Mama won't leave, then I'm going to. I can't stand it any more. I just don't care," I cried over the phone.

"Now, wait a minute. Where do you think you're going?" he asked.

"I don't know. Anywhere is better than this," I said.

"Why don't you come here for a few days and we'll figure something out?" he suggested. "You can stay with me and my mother. I'm sure she won't mind when I tell her why."

"I've never driven out of Harlan County. I don't know if I can make it to Ohio," I said. "I've never driven on the interstate."

"Call me back in a minute," he said.

We hung up the phones. I waited ten minutes and called him back.

"Look, if you can make it to Lexington where I-75 starts, my sister and I will meet you. I'll drive your car on up to Ohio. That's the best I can do on short notice," he said. "Are you sure you want to do this?"

"Listen here, I'm leaving no matter what. Tell me where and what time to meet you. I'm not even going back home for clothes. I just don't care," I said.

"I'm giving you plenty of time. We'll meet you at the service station right where I75 begins around two o'clock. You can't miss it," he said. "Be careful."

I felt such a relief. Someone was going to help me. "I'll be there," I said.

After hanging up the phone, I rummaged in the glove compartment for an emergency blank check my mother kept hidden in between the pages of a small prayer booklet. I wrote a check for fifty dollars, signed my mother's name to it, and cashed it at the Bank of Harlan. There were insufficient funds in the account to cover the amount of the check. Luckily, the bank vice-president, who happened to be a friend, called Mama later to fix the problem.

Finally having some control over my life, I drove out of Harlan County, leaving everything behind. Although I had a twinge of guilt leaving my mother, I knew that I could never change her mind. I was tired of trying to understand and give excuses for everything to everyone. I decided my future would not be based on my present, no matter what the consequences.

By reading an old map I found in the glove box, I drove to Lexington without a problem. Along the road, I stopped for gas and asked for directions just to make sure. Finding the meeting place was easier than I anticipated. Larry and his sister flagged me down as I pulled into the service station. Everything fell into place. After a quick introduction to his sister, he slid into the driver's seat of Mama's Studebaker, mentioning briefly that he could go to jail for transporting a minor across state lines. I didn't understand what he meant. His sister followed us in her car.

I watched him adjust the rearview mirror as if he was checking to see if we were being followed. He didn't say much but I felt his strength. With the speed of the car and the hot air blowing thru the open windows, I felt a new freedom. Driving through Cincinnati, the towering buildings captured my attention. I wondered how exciting it would be to live in a big city.

Reaching the outskirts of Hamilton, I reached over and hugged my boyfriend's neck. He smelled of English Leather, a far cry from Old Spice and bourbon. When we parked in front of his mother's apartment, his sister didn't stop. I had no fear meeting his mother simply because the unknown might prove to be better than what I had experienced. As it turned out, his mother was a gracious and kind woman.

"Susan, you really should call your mother and let her know that you are all right," she said. "I know if my child ran away, I would be crazy with worry."

"I don't know what to say to her," I said.

"You don't have to say anything you don't want to. Just give her a chance," she said. "You're welcome to stay here for a few days until you figure it out."

So with that piece of advice, I reluctantly called my mother. Hearing her frantic voice, I felt badly that I caused her so much anguish.

"Oh God, Susan, where are you?" Mama hollered over the phone. "Are you all right?"

"I'm fine. I'm in Ohio with Larry's family," I stated as a matter of fact. "I just couldn't stand it any longer."

"You drove to Ohio?" Mama asked.

Not wanting to get my boyfriend in trouble, I lied. "Yes, Mama, I drove."

"Honey, please come home. Your Daddy's here and we promise to do better if you'll just come back home," Mama pleaded.

"It's never going to get better," I answered. "I can't go on like this."

Mama handed Daddy the phone. "Honey, please come home. We'll work this out," Daddy sobbed. "I'm sorry."

With Mama back on the phone crying, I found it impossible to be cold-hearted. "Mama, I'm going to stay up here for a couple of days and then I'll come home. Maybe, it'll be different."

"Oh, honey, I love you. Please, please come home," Mama begged.

"I'll call you tomorrow night. I love you too," I sobbed.

The following day, I bought a pair of shorts and shirt for less than five dollars at a chain department store. Then Larry took me to my first putt-putt golf course and to the A&W Root Beer Stand, another first for me. In awe, it made me realize that someday I, too, could enjoy a normal life. In my mind, I stuffed my problems in a suitcase and threw them into the Ohio River. Somehow, I was going to make it.

The next evening I called Mama again. It was the same conversation. I didn't mean to hurt my mother. I was angry with her but I loved her. I agreed to come back home.

In the morning, my boyfriend's sister followed us from Hamilton, Ohio to Lexington, stopping off at the same service station. I thanked her, feeling somewhat embarrassed about the whole situation. I told Larry that he had a wonderful family and he should be grateful. They waved as I drove away, headed toward Harlan County once more.

Walking back into the house I called home felt somewhat embarrassed, maybe a little ashamed. My parents went overboard with their affection towards me as if I had been gone for months. I didn't enjoy my mother's behavior, actually feeling sorry for her. But I do confess that I relished my father's attention as it gave me a tremendous sense of power. As I had expected, the focus on the happy family life quickly came to an end. Once again, the whiskey bottle triumphed. Daddy moved back to

Lexington. I realized that the only control I garnered was of myself and to use the present to create the future. Only interested in graduating and getting on with my life, my senior year of high school slipped by quickly. I convinced myself that my future was in love and stability in my boyfriend.

CHAPTER TEN

To my mother's extreme disappointment and with the help of my father, I married my boyfriend a few months after high school graduation. Daddy revealed a part of himself that surprised and confused me. Maybe he did love me. He and my future mother-in-law drove Larry and me to Jellico, Tennessee where we exchanged vows in front a Justice of the Peace. I wore a blue linen dress, he wore slacks and short sleeve shirt. No frills, no flowers, no church. At the courthouse, I was offered the choice of getting married in a bank or a grocery store. I figured getting married in a bank would bring good luck. After the quickie wedding, I returned with my husband to Ohio to begin my life. We dined that evening at the Red Barn where we bought five hamburgers for one dollar. My wedding night was spent at my new sister and brother-in-law's house with their four young children. Still, I was happy.

Within a week, my new husband found a job and we moved into a small upstairs apartment near the railroad tracks inside the city limits of Hamilton. The rent, twenty dollars a week, was too high but we managed. Luckily, the electric, gas, water, and garbage were included in the rent. That gave us the luxury of having a phone as long as we were careful with our spending. Larry's wages averaged sixty dollars a week before taxes.

Mama surprised me, coming to visit soon after, buying most of the necessary household items: cookware, iron and ironing board, sheets, towels, utensils. I was ready to play house. I didn't realize at the time just how big a deal this was for my mother. She had never driven any farther than Lexington in her whole life.

The following year, I nearly died during childbirth. Although my son, Donnie, was born healthy, I lost too much blood. Daddy drove to the hospital and berated my doctor, pushing him up against the wall in a threatening way. Although this took place in my room, I barely remember the confrontation because I was so weak. When I was released from the hospital, Mama came to my rescue, staying at our apartment for the next two weeks to care for the baby since I was on bed rest until my health recovered.

Having had little contact with babies or caring for children, I relied heavily on my sister-in-law for advice. My *Dr. Spock Baby Care* book laid on my dresser, available to me at a moment's notice. Daddy visited often for the first several months, sleeping on a divan in our tiny apartment with his bottle. He never showed any aggressive behavior and, for that, I was thankful. He finally told me that he had moved from Lexington to Covington, Kentucky. He avoided any questions as to what kind of work he was doing in the city that nestled against the Ohio River across from Cincinnati. I didn't really care. Each time before he left, he pressed a twenty dollar bill in my hand. Our groceries went from twelve dollars a week to fifteen dollars a week when the baby came. So I appreciated the cash. I hid any extra change in a jar under the bed to buy Christmas presents. So for my first Christmas with my child, I saved a total of seventy-eight dollars, enough to buy Santa Claus, and give presents to both sides of the families. I was so proud.

It seemed that although the trip to Harlan took most of the day, we always ended up returning to the mountains at least for a weekend every couple of months. Mama beamed with pride over her grandchild. Our visits were good.

Several months later, I got a huge shock during one of my regular Sunday phone calls to Mama. She announced that she filed for divorce. *Why now, after I've been gone for nearly two years,* I wondered. "Mama, I don't understand. He lives hours away in Covington now. I thought everything was okay," I said. "What happened?"

"He still comes back. I think he's going to kill me," Mama explained. "I'm going to stay at Granny's until the divorce is final. I've got a lot of decisions to make. All I know right now is that I have to get out."

"When are you going to tell him?" I asked.

"He knows," Mama said. "So I think it would be a good idea if you didn't come home until this is over. There's no telling what he might do. He keeps threatening to burn the house down and I just tell him to go ahead. If you need to reach me, call up at Granny's. All I told her was that I was getting a divorce, nothing else. So don't you say anything more, okay?"

I agreed and stayed away from Harlan County until the dust settled. Stunned by this revelation, that after twenty-five years of marriage hell, and seventeen years of my life wasted, my dear mother had decided the time had come for a change, I wanted to scream; to demand a bigger and better reason. What was so different now? Was it because I left home, that I wasn't there to referee? What made her think that now he was going to kill her?

Fortunately, with the exception of a few threatening phone calls, Mama's divorce became final and she moved back home. Daddy relinquished the house and all assets to my mother.

His visits with me became fewer, not that I minded, except for the extra money part. Then I didn't hear from him nearly two months. Although he refused to give me his phone number, he usually managed to call me from a pay phone when he planned to visit. After a time, I wondered if somebody killed him. I still didn't know what he was doing for a living.

Then I receive another big surprise, again by telephone. I didn't know whether to laugh or cry.

"Susan, your Daddy is in Oklahoma," Mama began. "He called me late last night and asked me if it was okay if he got remarried. I told him I didn't give a damn."

"Wha . . . ?" I stuttered. "What's he doing in Oklahoma? How did he get out there? Who in the hell would marry him?"

"He told me he went out there on the Greyhound to visit his cousin, Mildred. You know he spent a lot of his childhood out there. Anyway, I never told you this but after your Daddy was discharged out of the Army after the World War II, we stayed several months in Vinita before moving back to Harlan. During that time, we became friends with a couple. We enjoyed their friendship as I didn't know too many people out in that dust bowl of a place. I hated it out there but just having a girlfriend was a big help. I really liked Wilma, she was a good person," Mama explained. "I might have even stayed out there if it hadn't been for Mildred. She made it unbearable for me. She was so jealous, wanting your father to herself."

After a pause, she continued, "So to make a long story short, your Daddy and Mildred visited Wilma after all this time and found out that she was divorced. So, your Daddy and Wilma are getting married or they may already be married. I just don't understand why she would marry him."

I really had no response, waiting for my brain to absorb the history, the present, and the future. After we hung up, I burst into tears, not really understanding why. Having no way of talking to my father, I had to wait until he contacted me. It wasn't long.

Within a week Daddy called, his voice upbeat, chattering like he was having the time of his life. I told him that Mama had called me earlier with the news. I don't know why he felt like he needed to explain, but he detailed the events leading up to the marriage, reiterating that his new wife was a good Christian woman. *So is my mother and look what you did to her,* I wanted to shout. Actually, I didn't say very much, I didn't have to. He said they would like to visit soon, to introduce her to me. Reluctantly, I agreed.

The following month, Daddy and Wilma drove from Oklahoma to Ohio for a three day visit. They stayed at a local motel because of lack of room in our one bedroom apartment. I felt relieved since the situation was awkward enough. At first, I thought my mind was playing tricks on me as I stared at Wilma, seeing unmistakable features just like my own mother. She carried a black and white picture of my mother and her taken in their younger days which she kindly gave me. The two women in the photo looked like sisters. *No wonder Daddy was drawn to her,* I thought.

The visit was strange. My stepmother proved to be all the good things that my parents said. With that in mind, I honestly felt sorry for her. I noticed during our time together that she showered Daddy with attention, even patting him on the knee, sitting close to him in a restaurant. He sucked it up like a wet noodle. *Mama might have been more attentive if he hadn't beat her to a pulp nearly every single night for twenty-five years*, I pondered, watching the two newlyweds coo. It made me sick.

Within the next couple of years, I rode the Greyhound to Oklahoma for two days and one night for a visit. I was shocked to see their nice brick home on the lake, a far cry from my childhood home. Daddy enjoyed showing off his grandson at a Indian Reservation, having his picture taken perched on the back of a stuffed buffalo. Nearby, a neighbor who bore an incredible resemblance to Colonel Sanders, kept small ponies on his ranch. One afternoon, we visited the ranch and my son had the opportunity to ride one of the ponies. Then another day, Daddy drove us to the Will Rodgers Museum in Claremore. Although he continued to drink excessively, nearly a fifth of bourbon a day, he never appeared drunk. Then, again, I had never seen him sober. I noticed during my visits that he never showed any violence toward his wife. Wilma never seemed bothered by anything other than his drinking which he never attempted to hide anyway.

Cousin Mildred continued to have an unhealthy influence on him. He thought of her like a sister since he was an only child. He listened to her intently and sought her approval on every aspect of his life. Once again, I felt concern for Wilma.

There were random phone calls between Daddy and I for the next few years. Once by car and once by bus, I visited their home. It appeared that life was good for my father and his wife, despite the liquor. I never pried into Daddy's life in Oklahoma nor did I want to. I was happy he was so far away.

Mama seemed to be content, still working at the same job, finding the time to enjoy a lunch with friends on occasion. Prior to her divorce, Mama's life encompassed her home, her job, and her faith. Becoming fiercely independent, she told me more than once, "I wouldn't have another man if he was handed to me on a silver platter. I like my life the way it is." I believed her.

In the meantime, as with most teen-age marriages, my six-year wedded bliss came to an end. In the late spring of 1974, I made a phone call to my dear mother. "Mama, can I come home?"

"Well, sure. When?" Mama asked.

"I mean for good," I explained. "Just me and Donnie."

"What's wrong?" she asked.

"Oh, Mama, I don't want to talk about it right now," I cried. "We'll leave early in the morning."

"All right. Just be careful!" she said. "I love you!"

"I love you too!" I said before hanging up the phone.

The only reason for my failed marriage was immaturity and a lot of stupidity on both sides. By middle afternoon that next day, I parked in front of the house I grew up in, my son sitting beside me in the front seat, ready to start a new life. I knew it wasn't going to be easy.

The next few weeks I was determined to not return to Ohio, rejecting my husband's pleas for another chance. I had no plans, no direction, no money. I did have my mother, however, I recognized the need to become independent.

"Look, honey, you have to do something with your life. As I see it, I can talk to the owner about hiring you as waitress at Creech Drug Store, or you can apply for loans and grants to go to the community college. It is your choice," Mama offered.

I knew she was right. Terrified of being hired and fired on the same day as a waitress, I chose college. Mama was pleased.

I eventually called Daddy, giving him the quick version of my divorce. I expected him to question or admonish me. Instead, he listened, and at the end of my prepared speech he said he was sorry. I didn't know what to think.

"What you going to do?" Daddy asked.

"Well, I've applied for some loans and grants. If I get those, I'm going to go to the community college. Donnie will be in school the same time I will be so it would work out. Then when I graduate, I'll hunt for a good job of some kind. Really, Daddy, I can't think that far," I explained.

"What about your mother?" he asked. "Let me tell you something my father told me, that two women cannot live in the same household. It has nothing to do with love either."

"She said we could live here," I answered. "I filed for something called public assistance to have some money for childcare after school on some days. Mama said she would let me use her new Dodge to drive back and forth. She bought an old clunker we nicknamed "Ol' Blue" for her to drive to work.

"You sound like you have everything worked out," he said. "Now, listen here, when you start looking for a job, try to get one with the government. I know you can't think of it right now but someday you'll want to retire and this is the way to go. I'm still barbering on the side but I'm working in a government children's home right now as a recreational director. It's got all kinds of benefits and a good retirement. Just keep what I said in mind."

Daddy had never talked to me at such a great length on personal matters. I guess I never knew he had any opinions except about a fifth of bourbon. When I hung up, I felt that I had finished a conversation with a counselor, not the man I called Daddy.

The next two years brought friction between Mama and me, so bad that sometimes we wouldn't speak to each other. The harder she tried to keep me on the righteous path, the harder I steered clear. Daddy never offered to help me financially, placing a burden on Mama that I couldn't alleviate. Nevertheless, after two long years, I graduated with over a three point average. I started working on August 1, 1976, as a Kentucky state employee. At the same time, I met a man who won my mother, my grandmother, and my son's approval. Despite the fact that Bill was the true classic redneck and I was the hillbilly hippie, I found stability, honesty, and a love of his gentle nature. When he asked my mother for permission to marry me, she had only one provision, that he not take me and Donnie out of Harlan County until after she died. I was twenty-seven years old. Bill made and kept that promise. I felt that Mama was glad that I moved out of her house. However, since we were just down the street, Donnie could go back and forth between homes. I called Daddy with the news. His response was polite, somewhat cool, as if I dug myself another hole to crawl out of.

A few weeks later, Daddy called inviting us to meet him in Somerset, Kentucky. "Daddy, why in the world would you be coming to Somerset?" I asked, completely confused.

"Well, I know this is a surprise. My mother, Laura, and her second husband, Hugo, who have been living in Detroit all these years, decided to move back to Somerset. That's where her family is from and she's still got a three sisters and a brother still living there. They're living on the same street that her sisters live. She wants to see me. I thought it would be nice if you all could meet them. I'd like to meet your new husband and see the little feller. We're going to stay at a local motel. I'll make you a reservation if you want me to. I'll pay for it," Daddy said.

"You said you'd pay for it? Did I hear you right?" I asked. "Daddy, I don't know what to say. I'll call you back tonight and you can give me all the details, okay?"

We did go to Somerset and we did meet the kinfolk. Before leaving, I mentioned briefly to Mama where we were going and why. We agreed that Donnie would stay with her for the weekend because it was going to be strange enough. He didn't care. She said that Daddy's mother had sneaked into the county to see me one time after I was born. I asked her what was the story about Daddy's mother and father. She refused, saying, "Go ask them."

I tried to prepare myself for the reunion, I tried to prepare Bill for the unknown . . . and the known. The drive was uneventful, with no problem finding the little garage apartment. We parked our old car beside Daddy's new Mercury. After hugs and introductions, I explained my son's absence due to prior plans. Then I quickly changed the subject.

"Daddy, I see that you've got another new car," I acknowledged. "Looks like you get one every time I turn around."

"Yeah, I'm playing it smart," he answered.

"What? The car is just getting broke in by that time. It's got a lot of mileage to go before you'd have to trade," I explained.

"No, you don't understand. You see, I trade for a new one every two years before something happens and it has to be repaired. That way I'm saving money. I don't have the expense of buying new tires or the chance of an oil leak. I just get a new car," he boasted.

I just smiled. *You are stupid. I'll bet you my bottom dollar that your cousin talked you into this,* I thought.

The atmosphere was uncomfortable. My grandmother's behavior was little more than politeness to a stranger, even to Daddy. But under the circumstances, it could have been worse. As soon as I saw her I caught myself staring, the resemblance between her and Daddy was undeniably obvious. I was amazed by her porcelain skin, no sign of a wrinkle. Her delicate white hands with slender fingers were a deep contrast to my poor Mama's reddened chapped hands. I whispered to Daddy what I observed. His response was, "Honey, that woman's never had a worry in her life." I didn't have time to ask him what he meant.

Grandma Laura's second husband, Hugo, proved to be a wonderful surprise. Of Finnish descent, he had a delightful accent, capturing my attention quickly. He apparently did all the household chores, including the cooking, and he was an accomplished carpenter.

After all this time, it was somewhat fruitless for Daddy to ask his mother, "What have you been doing all these years?" Yet, Daddy seemed happy, even when he stepped outside the apartment to take a swig of whiskey he stashed in the trunk of the car.

He welcomed Bill into this dysfunctional family. Wilma appeared all smiles. It seemed to be a happy event, a screwed up bunch who pretended nothing was wrong. Daddy bragged to his mother how my childhood was wonderful, that I had everything a little girl could ever want. He talked about the good times we had at the lake fishing, the great birthday parties I had been given.

I kept silent simply because I didn't know what to say . . . that the man sitting next to me was a liar. I had plenty to say back at the motel.

"Oh God, he's crazy. The liquor's finally caused him to lose his mind. I didn't know who he was talking about," I ranted, pacing around the bed, waving my arms.

"Settle down now. What difference does it make?" Bill asked.

"It makes a big difference to me! All those years? The pain he caused? He is either lying through his teeth for his mother to love him or he really believes what he is saying. Either way, it's nuts!" I cried. "I'd love to tell his mother all the misery he put us through."

"Now, you know you can't do that. She's an old woman," my husband said.

"Another thing, what's all this crap about wonderful birthday parties? I can't even remember any of my birthdays. Where's he getting all this stuff?" I fussed.

The night was long. Daddy came to our room with his bottle. I was nice, pretending once again. He challenged Bill to a drinking contest. I would have put money on my father, knowing he was a bottomless pit when it come to alcohol. However, my husband matched him drink for drink for several hours until Daddy said he needed to check on Wilma who was resting back in their room. For some reason, I was thrilled. I realized that Daddy had been drinking all day before they started the contest so Bill had an easy win. I thought this was one time Daddy had to admit defeat, but no, he used his wife as an excuse to quit.

The next day, Sunday, was the same banter. Daddy was in such a jovial mood, no signs of a hangover. I gritted my teeth, playing along. Before leaving, I hugged, kissed, and laughed, putting forth the best behavior I could muster. I hated myself. After waving a cheerful good-bye from our car, I crawled over the front seat and laid down in the back seat.

"What's wrong?" my husband asked. "Are you sick?"

"Oh God, yes, I'm sick, sick to death," I sobbed. "What was that back there? It was like I didn't even know myself. Everything Daddy talked about was a lie. Now that he's got such a great life in Oklahoma, he thinks the past just disappeared. Or, he's decided that if he tells enough lies, then sooner or later I'll believe it."

"Honey, I don't know. I can't tell you because I wasn't there years ago. But just remember that I love you, your Mama and Granny loves you, and your son loves you. That's all you need," my good husband said.

"I'm going to close my eyes. Let me know when we get home," I mumbled. "It'll be all right."

CHAPTER ELEVEN

For several years, I played my father's game. Each time he came to Somerset to visit his mother, I went along with his fantasies, waiting on a revelation of truth if only by accident. Sadly, Hugo passed away unexpectedly in the early 1980's. I wished I had gotten to know him better. After a fall resulting in a broken hip, Grandma Laura moved to a ground floor apartment for safety. Her general health was good, her mind sharp as a tack.

During one particular visit in Somerset, Wilma and I sat on the little front porch together while the others were talking in the living room. We rarely got time alone.

"You know, Susan, I wish your Daddy wouldn't drink so much. He really is a good man but the devil has a hold of him," she whispered. "I have been praying so hard for God to intervene. If he doesn't stop, he's going to kill himself in the car or die of a heart attack."

"I know," I said, nodding. "You have no idea what it was like."

"Oh, I think I have a good idea," she said. "I've tried talking to him but it doesn't help."

"I'm sorry," I said, looking away from her to keep from crying. "This sounds crazy but that man in there isn't the man I grew up with. I hardly know that man even though he looks like my Daddy. You have no idea what my mother went through."

"Honey, I love your mother. She's a good woman and was my best friend at one time," she said.

"I know. Mama told me. She hopes you don't have to live like she did," I said.

Our little talk ceased as Daddy came out on the porch to light a cigarette and take a break from the chatter inside the apartment. Laura's sisters never failed to join the visit which led to several conversations going on all at the same time.

Daddy's health continued to be good. He bragged that he never had a headache or a stomach ache in his life. I always responded, "No wonder, your stomach is pickled and your head is empty. Nothing there to hurt!" He would just laugh it off. I was serious.

All this pretense continued for years. When Grandma Laura turned ninety-one, she and her sisters decided to sell their belongings and move into a local nursing home. Of course, I only learned this after the fact by a phone call from Daddy. The only real change was the scenery, the visits remained the same.

Late one night, Daddy called me at home, so drunk I didn't even know it was him at first. His speech slurred so badly I asked him several times what he wanted. Finally, he screamed at me over the phone to look in my phone book and give him the number of one of his old lawyer friends. He wanted to call his buddy.

"Daddy, do you know what time it is?" I asked, thumbing through the pages for the phone number. "You're going to wake him. It's after midnight here."

"Give me the damn number," he spouted.

I repeated the phone number three times before he got it right and even then I didn't know for sure.

"Daddy, I'm hanging up now. I'm going back to bed," I said impatiently. "I've got to go to work in the morning."

"Oh, okay, nite nite. Bye," he mumbled and hung up the phone.

The next evening, I called Daddy back. "I just called to see if you were all right. Did you call your lawyer buddy?" I asked.

"What are you talking about?" he asked.

"You know, remember you called me last night wanting a phone number for him," I reminded him. "Don't you remember?"

There was a pause over the phone, then he replied, "No, honey, I don't remember."

The rest of the conversation was awkward as if he was trying to recall the night before but didn't want me to know he blacked out.

Two weeks later, I called again and Wilma answered the phone. "Susan, your Daddy's drinking is getting worse since he retired. He won't listen to me, says I'm preaching to him," she said softly. "I've been praying for him. I know God hears my prayers. I need to be more patient, I guess."

"Where is he right now?" I asked.

"He's sitting out on the screened in porch watching a western with his bottle of whiskey," she answered. "He's been out there all day, talking to the neighbors, telling jokes, making them laugh."

"Well, just don't tell him that I called. I'm so sorry, I really am," I said. "Maybe you could ask Mildred to talk to him. He seems to do everything she says anyway."

"I thought about that but I would really have to bite my tongue," she said. "You know, she treats me the same way she treated your mother, just insanely jealous of anybody close to your Daddy. I look at your Daddy and remember how he use to be. A lot of people still like him but they just see that one side of him, the funny side. I think God put him on this earth to make people laugh. The bottle shows his bad side. He's really a good man. I just wish I knew how to help him."

I didn't dare ask if he was violent with her as he had been with my mother The fact was that I didn't want to know. I had a hard time dealing with the past, I couldn't deal with the present.

It was nearly two months before I called again. I was not prepared for the news my stepmother gave me. Never in all my dreams and wishes did I ever think I would hear the words she spoke.

"Susan, your Daddy stopped drinking . . . and gave up the cigarettes too, at the same time. God gave us a miracle," she sobbed. "God answered my prayers."

Being extremely skeptical and wondering if Daddy had driven her crazy, I said, "Now, honey, wait a minute and think of what you're saying."

"It's true!" she said. "He's not had a drink or a cigarette in nearly five weeks. Praise God!"

"How did he do it?" I asked. "He's close to sixty-five years old and been drinking for at least fifty years. Are you sure he's not pulling the wool over your eyes?"

Wilma laughed, "Yes, I'm sure. Your Daddy is sober! The only help he needed was from God."

"But, I don't understand. What happened?" I asked. "Did he go to the doctor or to a hospital?"

She began, "It was on the weekend. He'd been drinking since early morning. It was around nine at night. He was sitting at the kitchen table and I was on the couch reading. He got up to go to the bathroom, stumbling all over the place. After all these years, he got confused and went into his bedroom. I heard a noise and ran to find him laying inside his closet with clothes and hangers all over the floor. I asked him if he was okay and he didn't answer. I got scared, thought he might be dead. I called Mildred and she drove out to the house. He was still laying in the closet when she arrived. I couldn't believe what happened. Mildred said, "Good Lord, Quinton, what are you trying to do, kill yourself? Get up out of there and stop this right now. I'm so ashamed of you!" To my surprise, your Daddy pulled himself up and walked back into the kitchen without a word. He poured the rest of the bourbon down the sink and went to bed. Mildred and I sat for a long time on the couch, unable to speak. She finally left and then I went to bed. The next day, your Daddy never touched a drop of liquor. I held my breath. I was afraid to say anything, afraid I would burst out crying. He stayed in bed a lot for the next few days but never asked for a drink or a smoke. I even checked under his bed, in the bathroom, under the sink, even in the closets and found no whiskey. After a couple of weeks, he seemed to emerge the same person I knew years ago, a good man with a kind heart. I give thanks to the Lord every day and night. I know he could fall back anytime but I put my trust in the Lord and He will see us through."

Difficult to believe her wild tale, I asked, "Where is he right now?"

"He's laying down taking a nap but I'll get him to call you when he gets up. I wanted to tell you sooner but he wanted to wait. I think he's embarrassed," she said.

After we hung up I turned to my husband. "Daddy's quit drinking."

"Yeah, sure. Who said that?" Bill asked, dripping in sarcasm.

"Wilma! She said God gave her a miracle. Daddy quit . . . just like that," I said, snapping my fingers. "He's going to call me later but right now I'm going to run down to Mama's and tell her."

Relaying the story to my mother, watching her facial expressions change from a frown to a smile didn't prepare me for her reaction.

"Susan, don't be ridiculous. That S.O.B. has just got her fooled. I don't believe it for one minute, do you?" Mama laughed as she puffed on her cigarette. "Don't be so gullible."

"Mama, I don't know. I'm only telling you what was told to me," I explained, feeling a little stupid that I even considered it to be real.

I left my mother's house less shocked and more depressed. If Daddy was pulling a scam, then it would come out eventually. If God truly worked a miracle, I will finally get to know my father without the shadows, the worries, and the fears. I wondered if now he remembered the nightmare we lived. I hoped so.

Later that night, Daddy called. "Yep, I did it, no problem, right off the bat. Haven't had a drink in about five weeks. I thought about keeping my cigarettes til later but no, I just put them down at the same time," Daddy bragged. "Funny thing though, I ain't had a craving for neither one."

"Don't you think God had something to do with it, Daddy?" I said, gritting my teeth. *You are so full of it*, I thought.

"Oh, sure, sure. You know my wife has a direct line to the Man upstairs," he said.

"How do you feel?" I asked, not knowing whether to believe a word he said.

"I feel just fine. In fact, I am thinking about opening up a little barbershop on up the road just to keep me busy," he said. "I've still got my barbering tools. I know I'd get a good business, especially from all the farmers and retired people out here."

"Well, Daddy, that's great. I think you'd like that," I answered. "You sound so good over the phone. I'm really happy for you."

"I'm real happy for me too," he responded.

After we hung up, I sat on the couch in a daze. All these years, I sought out reality instead of dreams. I couldn't absorb the possibility of a teetotaling Daddy.

The following months were filled with increased phone calls with updates of Daddy's barbershop, new appliances for their homes, and another new car. It was as if the minute he stopped drinking, his life turned around bringing all good things to his doorstep. I tried very hard to be happy for him but deep down, I wanted to scream. After all this time, he continued to behave as if the past was the image of the television series, *Father Knows Best*. I felt selfish.

The years went by quickly. Daddy never took another drink. He boasted that two nearby liquor stores went out of business after he quit. In the late 1990's, Daddy called with a request. "Susan, instead of us meeting in Somerset for our visit, I'd like to come to Harlan to see you all. That is if it's okay with you and

Bill. Wilma isn't coming this time. The trip is so long and hard on her that she said she would rather just stay at home. Now if you think it will be a problem because of your mother, then I'll understand."

"No, no, it won't be a problem. Of course, I'll have to tell her you're coming but we won't even drive by her house," I blurted out, so surprised by his suggestion. "But I don't think there will any problem. Of course, you are welcome here and if Wilma changes her mind, that's fine too."

After I hung up, I realized what I had said. *How in the world am I going to pull this off? Mama is going to be furious with me,* I thought. *I don't really blame her.*

I thought about calling Mama, knowing that was the chicken way out. Bill said the right thing would be to go tell her in person, especially since she just lived two blocks away from us.

"Look, Susan, with your luck, if you didn't tell her that he was coming, you all would run into each other at the mall or something. That wouldn't be fair to her and you know it," my husband argued. "Go on down there and tell her right now so she'll have some time to get use to the idea. He's not been back to Harlan since they got divorced. Then again, maybe she won't care."

"Yeah, fat chance of that. He's probably been afraid to come into Harlan because of Mama," I said. "I don't blame him."

I walked slowly down to Mama's house, trying to think of the right words to say. Her hatred for my father was no doubt justified but I didn't want her to be mad at me. Once again I was caught in the middle.

I found her in the back yard planting some four o'clocks beside the back porch. "Hi Mama. Can you stop and rest for a minute? I've got some news."

"Susan, I'm busy. My hands are in the dirt. Can't you tell me while I finish this?" she asked, not even looking up from her job.

I took a deep breath. "Mama, Daddy is coming for a visit next week."

"I don't give a damn. When will you be back, Sunday evening?" she asked.

"No Mama, he's coming here, to Harlan," I stuttered. "I mean he's staying at our house."

I watched Mama's back stiffen as she raised back and stood up. Giving me a look that could kill, she grabbed a rag and wiped her hands. "Let's go into the house," she ordered.

We sat at the kitchen table. "Mama, please don't be mad at me. I didn't know what else to tell him when he asked. It wasn't my idea, honestly," I said.

"That's just fine. I don't know how you can stand that sorry thing but if you want him in your house then go right ahead," Mama ranted. "I just can't believe he's got the nerve to show his face. You know, he didn't even come to his own father's funeral and that's been more than twenty years ago. He never did do anything for you growing up either."

"I know that," I said, not wanting to say anything else to make it worse. "Okay, Mama, I'm going to go now and I'll see you tomorrow."

"When did you say he was coming?" she asked, wiping the sweat off of her forehead.

"He said next week. I'll let you know what day and how long he's staying as soon as I know," I answered, going out the door.

"Good. I guess I'll have to stay in my house the whole time he's here," Mama hollered.

"Mama, he's an old man now. What in the world could he do?" I yelled back.

Walking back to my house, my thoughts rambled, *In the first place, if Mama had left when I was little, maybe our lives would have been for the better. But noooo, she had all these reasons that didn't amount to a hill of beans. I know she hates him, but to beat it all, it seems like she blames me.*

Donnie was then out of college and living in Florida. I didn't bother him with details of the drama. I knew he would never understand. After talking to Daddy once more, I relayed his plans to Mama. I arranged to take some vacations days off from work. All was done but the waiting.

Daddy found a safer way of driving from Oklahoma to Somerset by using two lane roads nearly all the way. It took a few hours longer but it was easier for him. He came up with the idea after one trip when he missed a ramp in St. Louis and jumped the median going the wrong way. He said horns blew and drivers flipped him the bird while moving out of his way. He smiled, waving back.

From Somerset to Harlan was about two and a half hours. He planned to stop and see his mother there and then drive on to Harlan. I didn't worry about him because I decided a long time ago that God had to have an army of angels watching over him. One would never be enough.

The afternoon that he parked his fancy New Yorker in our driveway, I ran out the back door to greet him. I thought he would be nearly paralyzed driving so many hours and I was prepared to give him a helping hand to get out of the driver's seat. I should have known better. He bounded out of the car like a thirty-year-old, making me feel like I was falling apart already.

"Daddy, you made it!" I hollered, giving him a big hug.

"Of course, I did. Did you have any doubts?" he chuckled. "It was an easy drive. I didn't have a bit of trouble."

We sat at the kitchen table as I poured him a glass of water. "Daddy, you really look good. How's Wilma?"

"She's just fine. I have to call her in a minute. I promised to let her know when I got here," he said, handing me his car keys. "Go out to the car and get those sacks out of the trunk. I'll get my clothes later. Where's your phone?"

"Okay. The phone is in the living room on the table right beside the couch. Take your time. Do you need help getting up?" I asked.

"For heaven sakes, you act like I'm old or something," he said. "Go on!"

I got the paper sacks out of the trunk as he requested. He had a very old small Samsonite suitcase, four shirts and two pairs of pants on hangers, and a pair of dress shoes. I figured he planned on staying three or four days. He hadn't said and I hadn't asked.

After reporting to his wife, he joined me back in the kitchen. He opened the sacks, laying out on the table several trinkets, a cup and saucer, some costume jewelry, and a Oklahoma cap. "I bought this jewelry for you when I stopped to gas up in Missouri. The cup and saucer come from my cousin. She thought you would like to have it. Wilma went through the house and found these trinkets for you," he boasted, running his hand over the gifts. This cap's for Bill. I figured he'd still be working. Oh, honey, it's so good to see you."

"Thank you, Daddy," I said, cheerfully. "Yes, but he'll be home about six o'clock. He's bringing some burgers and fries from Dairy Queen, if that's okay with you?"

"That's just fine. I don't expect you to cook anyway," he said. "Now while we're sitting here, let's just get something out of the way. I'm only going to stay a couple of days. That's long enough," he said. "My Daddy always said that company was like fish, after three days they start to stink. I don't want to stink!"

I laughed. "You know you can stay longer than that. You just got here."

"Does your mother know I'm here?" he asked.

"Yes, why?"

"Here's what I got in mind and don't give me a hard time about it either. You call her and see if I can come down and talk to her tomorrow just for a few minutes," he whispered even though we were the only two in the house.

"Are you sure you want to do this?" I asked, reeling from his suggestion. "Are you crazy?"

"Yes. If she says no, I don't blame her," he said.

With Daddy sitting beside of me on the couch, I called my mother. Not knowing how to ease into the proposal, I just blurted it out as if it was an everyday event. Daddy rolled his eyes. At first her silence gave me reason to think she hung up on me but she finally spoke, giving him permission to come to her house at two o'clock the next day.

CHAPTER TWELVE

I found Daddy sipping a cup of coffee at the kitchen table early the next morning. Knowing how stressed I felt, Bill hadn't wakened me before going to work.

"Good morning, Daddy. How long have you been up?" I asked, pulling my hair back from my face.

"Oh, I've been awake for a long time. I heard Bill in the kitchen so I got on up. No sense in just laying in the bed," he said. "I don't need much sleep."

"Did you sleep well in Donnie's room? Was the bed okay?" I asked, sitting down at the table.

"Oh, I slept like a log," he answered. "It's just when it gets daylight, it's time to get up. I guess the one hour time difference could be another reason. I didn't even think about that until now."

"Well, what do you want to do today? I mean, before you go to Mama's house," I said.

"I was thinking about that last night. If it's all right with you, I want us to stop by the Catholic church for a few minutes," he suggested. "Then if we got time, we can just drive around through town. I want to see all the old places, like the Cumberland Barber Shop and the Courthouse. I remember sitting with my father on one of those benches in front of the Courthouse when I was a little boy. He was always good to me."

"Daddy, what happened back then?" I dared to ask. "You never have told me anything."

A deep sadness washed over his face. "Not now, Susan. Maybe, someday," he said weakly.

By the time Daddy finished showering and shaving, I was dressed and waiting. He looked good in his blue jeans and red checkered shirt. He even sported a cowboy hat which soon became more cumbersome than fancy. I noticed he was wearing a different kind of cologne.

Where's your Old Spice?' I asked, sniffing as he walked into the living room.

"I left it at home. Mildred told me to pack the new cologne she gave me last Christmas. I saw it advertised on television," he said. "What do you think?"

"No, you're just fine. You smell real good. Are you ready to go?" I asked.

"Yep, do you want to drive my car?" he asked, digging in his pockets for his keys.

"No, let's go in my car. I'd be scared to death to drive your car, afraid I would hit something," I chuckled. "Way too big for me."

We didn't say much on the drive to the little church that played such a big part of our lives. I had mixed feelings, my stomach churned trying to make sense of Daddy's sudden interests after so many years. I parked the car in front of the steps.

"Does your mother still go to church here?" he whispered.

"Yes, every time the doors are open," I replied. "She's never stopped."

"Would you go in with me?" he whispered. "You know, me and your mother were some of the first parishioners at Holy Trinity. Do you remember when the church was built?"

"Yes, Daddy, I'll go in with you but you don't have to whisper. There's no one else in the car but us," I said.

As we walked up the steps my body trembled with emotion. Daddy opened the door for me. Although my mother went to church faithfully, I only attended occasionally. Having two marriages without the Catholic Church's blessing presented problems such as not being able to receive Communion and other Sacraments. Because Daddy had remarried while my mother was still living, the Catholic Church frowned upon him as well.

"When you go in, be very careful," he said. "With the both of us in here, the roof might fall in." He took my hand. "Come on, little girl."

"Hey, where's the two holy water fountains that were always in the back here? You know, one of them had our name on it and the other was donated by the McCreary's," he asked, looking around.

"Daddy, they took them out years ago. I don't know why. I don't even know what happened to them," I answered. "Maybe Mama can tell you."

We knelt in the same third row pew from the back and prayed. With his hands folded, he looked straight ahead to the altar. My prayer was short and to the point.

Dear God, Thank you for all Your blessings, especially for this one right now. I don't understand what's going on but I trust in You. Thank you again for giving Daddy a miracle. It was a miracle for all of us. Amen.

The sunlight filtered through the beautiful stained glass windows as we sat together in silence. I was so relieved when he wanted to go. Feeling lightheaded, I prayed that I wouldn't faint, especially in church.

I drove him into city, the streets changed now to mostly one-way. I parked in front of the Cumberland Barber Shop. Inside, we found one of his buddies who still worked there. It was a bittersweet reunion. It felt awkward as Daddy tried to reminisce since most of his memories during those years were clouded by liquor.

We walked over to the Courthouse and sat on a bench. He seemed to reflect on a world I knew nothing about. "You know, honey, when I was a little boy, the Salvation Army Band would play right here in front of the Doughboy Statue. Listening to their music, especially the tambourines, always fascinated me and my daddy," he said. "That was a long time ago."

Then, looking across the street over to the insurance office where Mama worked for more than thirty years, his sadness changed to shock. He squinted his eyes as if unsure of what he saw. "What happened over there? And look at Creech Drug? What happened? That used to be one of the finest buildings," he asked. "Now, when I look around, what happened to the town? Where's all the people?"

"Daddy, you've been gone a long time. It's changed," I said. "It's just not the coal booming town you remember. Everybody goes to the mall or Walmart."

Returning home, I drove slowly by Granny's house in Lawnvale.

"Susan, how'd your mother do when Granny passed away?" Daddy asked, truly concerned. "I know it must have been awfully hard on her."

"Well, Granny was ninety-eight and her health was really bad. Mama took care of her until she just couldn't. It nearly killed Mama when Granny went into the nursing home. But, honestly, Granny would have been dead a long time ago if hadn't been for Mama's dedication. I think Mama finally realized that it was time for Granny to go," I explained. "Now that the flood control project is coming in, the government will probably buy the house. You know it's been hit with every flood that I can remember."

At home, we ate ham sandwiches and chips. I was not one for cooking and he knew it. Afterwards, we sat on the couch looking at photo albums.

"Daddy," I paused, "What made you want to go to church this morning?"

He laughed and said, "Now, look here. I'm going to be stepping into a bear's den in a couple of hours and I need all the help I can get."

I should have known that he would make a joke out of it. I just let it go. He wasn't going to tell me anyway.

As the time neared, Daddy got sillier. "Do I need more deodorant? Come smell my armpits," he quipped, raising his arms. "You know your mother has a good nose." He looked down at his clothes. "Do I need to change clothes? Am I too wrinkled?"

"Yeah, Daddy, you stink and you're wrinkled . . . all over," I answered.

At five minutes before the agreed visit, I drove my nervous father down to see the woman he treated so badly for twenty-five years. Instead of us going in the back door, we walked up the steps to the front porch and rang the door bell. I almost laughed. Mama opened the door, looking like she stepped out of a magazine. She still had her petite figure, her salt and pepper hair was perfectly coiffed, and she was wearing a flattering print dress. This was the first time she had seen Daddy since he left and she shined. Daddy, on the other hand, weighed in at least 275 pounds. I stayed a few minutes for the pleasantries and to make sure Mama didn't kill him. Then I excused myself, saying I had to run to the grocery and I would be back in a couple of hours. Although I was uneasy about leaving them together, I had to take the chance. I could just envision the headlines in the *Harlan Daily Enterprise*, "Former Couple Arrested for Disturbance" with the subtitle, "Big man down as little lady takes a mighty swing."

Back at home, I called my husband for moral support. He assured me that if he heard on his scanner that the police were called to Mama's residence, he would let me know. He told me I was paranoid and I agreed, but with good cause. To pass the time, I washed a load of clothes, watched some television, drank two glasses of tea, ate six cookies, and paced the floors. I thought about taking a shower but then I wouldn't be able to hear the phone in case of an emergency.

At three forty-five, I couldn't wait any longer. I drove back down to Mama's house, prepared to pick up the remains of whatever had happened. I didn't bother knocking. Mama and Daddy were at the kitchen table, drinking coffee. I honestly didn't know how to carry on a conversation with the two of them together.

"Well, glad to see both of you alive. What did you talk about?" I asked both of them. *That's a stupid thing to say*, I thought.

"None of your business, Susan," Mama answered.

"Well, I guess we better be going," Daddy said, putting his cup in the sink. "Thank you for the visit and the coffee."

He turned to me. "Oh, Susan, I'd like to take everyone out to supper tomorrow evening. Your mother has agreed to go with us," Daddy announced.

"Uhhhh, okay. We can go to Western Sizzlin, that's about the only sit-down place to eat," I answered, nearly dumbfounded. I glanced at Mama for any reaction but found none.

"What time will Bill get off work?" Daddy asked.

"Usually he is home by five o'clock unless he works overtime. Let's plan on going at six and if something happens, we can always change it for later," I rambled. "Is that alright with you, Mama?"

"That's fine with me," Mama answered. "I'll be ready."

Daddy and I returned home in silence. I waited for an explanation. It was difficult keeping my mouth shut, just dying to know what they talked about. Daddy didn't even give me a hint. I would have to get it out of Mama, later.

The next day, Daddy was full of vim and vigor. "Today, how about we go see Mag? Is she still alive?" he asked.

"Why, Daddy, do you want to go there?" I asked, my heart pounding at the thought of visiting the local bootlegger after all these years.

"Now, honey, she's a sweet old woman. She always treated me and my daddy really good. You know, he use to take me to see her when I was a little boy," he said. "Always wore an apron, every single time."

Daddy saw a sadness wash over my face. I frowned.

"Oh, it's not to buy any whiskey. I promise you that. I'll just go in and say hello," he said. "Don't worry. That part of my life is over."

Reluctantly, I drove to Clovertown, parked behind Mag's house and got out of the car before she came outside. Daddy knocked. Mag opened the back door.

Daddy stood there with the biggest grin on his face. "Do you remember me, Mag?"

Mag stood there, squinted her eyes, studying the man in front of her. "Now wait a minute. Oh, my goodness, Quinton Noe! I thought you were dead. Come on in here. My sister's in the living room."

"This is my daughter, Susan," he said. "I'm here visiting and wanted to come by for a minute."

Daddy didn't know that in my younger days, I frequented Mag's quite a bit. Of course, with all the customers Mag had through the generations, it was impossible for her to remember all of them. Daddy was special, I guess.

We stayed about fifteen minutes before Daddy suggested we leave. It was a nice visit and Daddy kept his promise, no whiskey.

As we went by Granny's house again on the way home, Daddy suggested we go to Resthaven Cemetery. I had no problem with that. Besides, Daddy always said it was the only place where folks won't disagree with you. I agreed with that!

Since Mama's people were buried up on the hill, Daddy and I just sat in the car and talked. His knees were weak, not able to climb on steep ground.

Looking up at Granny and Granddaddy's grave marker, Daddy said, "I really loved that old woman. Granny was a good woman and a hard worker. She loved me. I liked your Granddaddy too. We use to sip homebrew from time to time."

I nodded, unable to think of a response. *Doesn't he remember running us off to the motel and blaming Granny for everything?* I thought. *Has he changed his whole past?*

"Now, Susan, don't get the wrong idea about tonight. Wilma's the one who suggested that I do this. She said it was the right thing to do. I agree. So don't think that I'm doing something I shouldn't be doing," Daddy said.

"I never thought that at all. It's weird, for sure. I could've fallen over dead when Mama said she would go," I said. "Does she believe now that you quit drinking?"

"I don't know. I don't blame her if she doesn't. She's a good woman, and she's been a good mother to you," he said. "I hope you appreciate her. She loves you so much . . . and that grandson is the light of her life."

I smiled, waiting in vain for some kind of admission of guilt, some kind of true personal acknowledgment of the horrible things he did, to my mother, to me. It didn't happen. Did he have selective memory? Was a stir into his past too difficult to recall? I didn't know.

At six sharp, Daddy drove up in front of Mama's house in his fine car. With Bill sitting in the front seat, Mama took her place in the back seat with me. That arrangement seemed appropriate. I smiled at my mother, she patted my hand. I didn't know if it felt like a reunion or a funeral. The men bantered the whole time. I figured it was a form of nervous chatter to prevent a weird silence.

Inside Western Sizzlin, we sat in the back avoiding as many patrons as possible. The service was good, the food was wonderful. At least that was what Bill said later. I could barely choke down my steak, my stomach in knots, my heart racing. Obvious politeness dictated the conversation, which at times, felt surreal. The past two days showed promise of a television comedy series or, on the other hand, a best-selling book. By the time we dropped off Mama back at her house, I was exhausted.

With his bag already packed and placed at the back door, Daddy was ready to leave early the next morning. Bill wished him well before he went to work. Honestly, I wanted Daddy to stay another day, but his plans were to stop back by and see his mother again before he headed to Oklahoma. I realized he had a desperate desire to reconnect with his mother, so I didn't press him to say in Harlan. Whatever he was looking for, he had to find it on his own. Besides, I was anxious to see what Mama had to say about all this.

I waited an hour after Daddy left to go see my mother. Collecting my thoughts and trying to carefully prepare a mental questionnaire, I opened Mama's back door as if I was entering the twilight zone. The tantalizing aroma nearly made me forget my mission. I found Mama at the stove, finishing a scrambled egg to go along with the two pieces of crispy fried bacon. A fresh buttered piece of toast made my mouth water.

"Honey, do you want me to fix you some?" Mama asked, obviously in a good mood. "It won't take but a minute."

"No, thanks, Mama, I've already eaten," I lied. "Daddy left this morning, going back to see his mother and then on home.

"Well, the old S.O.B. said he was only going to stay a couple of days. How was his visit with you?" she asked while filling her plate. She sat down at the kitchen table with me.

"It was fine . . . strange, but fine. I don't know how it's suppose to be, so I guess it was fine," I answered. "Okay, enough of the small talk. Tell me what you two talked about when he was down here the other day."

Mama set her fork down, took a sip of coffee, and with a deep breath, she began, "We talked about you and how lucky I was to have you live near me. We talked about our grandson and how proud we are of him. We also agreed how fortunate you were to have Bill."

"That's well and good. But didn't he say anything about the past, about what he did . . . to you, to me? Did he pretend just like he does with me?" I demanded a little too harshly.

"Now, look, Susan, I don't remember everything we talked about, and it's none of your business. But no, he didn't bring up the past. What's the point?" she replied.

"Well, the point is that he could've apologized to you or at least admitted how bad he was," I explained. "At least, it'd be better than what I get from him which is nothing but this happy, happy attitude. I hate it. We lived in pure hell."

Mama stopped eating, pushed her plate away, and closed her eyes for a second. "Susan, I'm truly sorry, really I am. I'm sorry that I didn't take you and leave him. I could have been a better mother. I'm sorry that you had to live like that and if I could do it over again, I'd do it different. I hate him so much for what he did to you and I hate myself too. You know that I love you more than anything in this world," Mama cried. "I was so afraid. I didn't know where to go or who to go to. I was afraid God would be angry with me. I didn't want my family to know what was going on. Your father said that if I left, he would kill me. He made me believe that I was useless, worthless, and couldn't make it on my own. And then, there was you, my little girl, and I was afraid for you too.

I knelt down beside her and put my arms around her. Tears flowed. For the first time, my mother acknowledged the terror we endured all those years. I realized that she was trapped . . . in fear, with intimidation, and lack of any support. "Mama, nooo, you did all you could at the time. It's not your fault, none of it. You know I love you," I sobbed. "Like you said, back then we had no place to go. I'm sorry too."

"He did say something that day. Right before you came, he told me he always loved me," Mama said, embarrassed. "I didn't know what else to say so I said, "Thank you." Isn't that the dumbest thing you've ever heard?"

"Well, no. Under the circumstances I think that was very kind of you. That's probably the closest to an apology that you'll ever get," I said.

137

"You're probably right," she said. "You know what I think? I really believe that he chooses not to remember. I can't see how in the world that he can just dismiss all those years but apparently, he can. Didn't he say anything to you?"

"No. As usual, it was jokes and what a happy life he has," I answered. "Oh, of course he mentions all the money he has. What I don't understand is where in the world does he get his money?"

"Honey, Mildred is well off and I am sure she takes good care of him," she answered. "You know he drank up every dime he made when he was in Harlan."

I stayed another hour, making sure Mama was okay before I returned home. For the first time, I understood my mother's intentions and her way of coping with the small town attitudes and rigid beliefs of that era. All the misplaced anger that I had felt toward my mother dissolved that day. She believed that she was doing the right thing, keeping the family together, no matter what the cost. My dear mother truly loved me.

CHAPTER THIRTEEN

Returning to work the next week, I found myself still thinking about Daddy's visit, his words to my mother, and my mother's
words to me. One day, while talking to a customer regarding her
unemployment benefits, the woman's husband became irate for
reasons unknown to me. He suddenly raised his hand as if to hit
her. Instantly, I felt a terror, a horrible sinking feeling as if I was
reliving the past. He caught himself before delivering the blow.
With a firm voice, I told the man to leave and sit up front. After
the couple left the office, I went into the bathroom and splashed
cold water on my face. I couldn't breathe. Feeling dizzy, I sat in
the stall for several minutes before returning to my desk. I said
nothing to my co-workers.

Several months later, Daddy called very unexpectedly with
news about his cousin. I heard a childlike sadness in his voice.
"Susan, I thought I would call and tell you that Mildred passed
away. It was her heart," he said softly. "You know, she'd just been
in the nursing home a few weeks. The last time I was there, she
grabbed my arm and whispered for me not to worry, that I would
be well taken care of. I told her to quit talking like that. Maybe
she knew she wasn't going to last long."

"Daddy, I'm so sorry. Do you need me to come out there?
When is the funeral so I can order flowers?" I asked.

"Oh, no, honey, I already buried her," he said quickly. "She's
in the ground. Wasted no time."

"What? You waited until you had the funeral to call and tell me?" I shouted. "Don't you think I would have liked to know?

"What could you have done? There was no point in telling you and have you come all the way out here for a funeral. Everything's taken care of. I've called someone to come and appraise her things and give me a price. I'm giving all her clothes, some still with price tags on them, to the Goodwill. She was so little, wore a size two. I don't know anybody that could wear her clothes. I bet she had forty pairs of shoes, all tiny sizes."

"Daddy, I think that is awful. You should have told me," I said. "Was there a funeral?"

"Yeah, I had a service for her. I even picked out what she wore. I just did it quick," he said proudly. "Besides, you didn't need to send flowers. Do you know how much they cost?"

"Dear Lord, I just can't believe this. You waited until she was in the ground before you call. Is that what is going to happen with you? Are you going to tell Wilma or someone to call and tell me after you are dead and buried?" I asked.

"Yeah, probably. When I'm dead, you can't do anything about it anyway so what's the difference?" he asked. "I just didn't want to bother you with details."

I was livid. Trying to be civil with my father proved to be too much of an effort. "Okay, Daddy, let me know if there's anything you want me to do. Since she was from Harlan, do you want me to put it in the paper here?" I asked.

"No, don't bother. She's been gone from there for years. Besides most of the people she knows are dead anyway. I just wanted you to know," he replied.

After we hung up, I sat on the couch absorbing the whole wacky conversation. I called Mama and told her of Mildred's passing. She said she would send flowers. That is when I told her . . . too late for that. Her response was that Daddy was crazy. I agreed.

A couple of weeks later, Daddy called to inform me that Mildred had wanted me to have her car, a fairly new Ford Taurus.

I readily accepted the offer. He drove the car to Harlan the next week, stayed until Friday. Bill took off of work for one day and we drove Daddy back to Oklahoma because he absolutely refused to take a plane. We traveled straight through, taking about fourteen hours. We stopped off at his house, spent some time with Wilma, and then checked in a local motel. The next day, Daddy took us to several places, including Big Cabin, a huge truck stop that my husband just loved. Late Saturday night, a storm moved in with large hail and wind.

At two a.m. on Sunday morning, we left Oklahoma in our new car, simply because we had no place to park the car out of the hail in the middle of the night. Daddy thought we were going to leave that morning anyway so I didn't think it was a big deal. Apparently, I was wrong because at daybreak, Daddy had driven out to the motel to take us to breakfast. I called him later and explained. He thought we were crazy. I asked him if he would have left his new car out to be pounded with hail. I think I insulted him.

Life seemed to improve as the years mounted. In the summer of 2000, my mother had a serious bout of bronchitis which seemed to linger. After a couple of weeks of my continuous nagging, she went to the doctor. With a round of antibiotics, her problem appeared to be healed. She loathed those who complained so it was very difficult to find her acknowledging a problem. However, she began to have severe pains in her stomach. She refused to go to the doctor, putting it off until November. At that time she was diagnosed with terminal cancer. I called my father with the devastating news. This was one of those times he was nearly speechless. In March 2001, two weeks before she passed away, I stayed with her in her home as she chose to die in the little house she loved. We talked about her feelings, laying to rest all the emotional baggage, the hatred and animosity toward the past and with herself. It was a healing process in the face of death.

"Mama, someday I'd like to write a book about all this, what we endured, what we learned," I mentioned carefully.

"I think that would be good. It might help somebody. You never know," she answered. "But there's one thing you have to promise me."

"What is that?" I asked.

"You have to promise me that you will not write or tell what happened until I'm dead," she said seriously. "I mean it."

"I promise, Mama," I answered softly. "Don't worry."

Each time Daddy called me, his voice was low, soft, but matter-of-fact. I wanted to scream through the phone, curse him, condemn him to an abyss of guilt. I wanted him to feel remorse, to beg forgiveness, to confess. I knew he didn't cause her cancer but I needed a scapegoat, even if only in my mind. I did call him after she died . . . before the funeral. They sent some beautiful flowers. I was determined not to behave as he did with Mildred.

There was standing room only in the little Catholic church that my mother loved so much. The beautiful funeral Mass exemplified the person she strived to be, a good Catholic, a good woman, and a good mother. Her house felt incredibly cold and empty. My heart felt the same way.

Five months after Mama died, I was held hostage and shot at work by a disgruntled retired co-worker. After my recovery, a friend asked me, "Did you change your life?" and I thought about that for a minute and replied, "No, my life changed." It was true. I realized that God had a plan for me and if I just allowed it, He would put me where He wants me. After continuing to work another year, I retired gracefully. It was a difficult decision leaving the people I had spent more waking time with over the years than my family, but I felt it was the right thing to do.

A few months later, Donnie surprised us with the news of wedding plans. Our first meeting with our future daughter-in-law proved to be a welcome sight. A blanket of snow covered a thin layer of ice overnight which failed to melt by the time

Donnie and his fiancé arrived at our home. We stood at the back door, curious for our first peek at the woman who stole our son's heart away. As she took a step around the back of their car, her feet flew out from under her and she landed on her bottom, hard. Bill looked at me and said, "Yep, there's our new daughter!"

Immediately, Bill and I felt a close connection with our future daughter-in-law. Donnie looked happier than we had ever seen him. Life was a roller coaster. In 2002, Bill and I watched our son marry a lovely young woman in the Virgin Islands.

My father and I continued to visit, sometimes twice a year. It continued to play out as a fictional story of happy reunions. In 2004, with Bill and me now retired, we decided to move to Florida to be near our son, daughter-in-law and new grandson. We sold our house and most of the furniture. We shipped seven large boxes by UPS and crammed everything we could get into our car for our new adventure. While in the midst of hurricane weather and signing papers to our new house, I got a phone call from Daddy.

"Susan, I just wanted to tell you that Laura died," Daddy said. "You know she was a hundred and four years old."

"Daddy, I'm so sorry. When is the funeral or have they already had it?" I asked, holding my cell phone to my ear while signing the dotted line.

"It's in a couple of days. I don't think I can go, my knees are getting really bad and Wilma's been pretty sick," he said. "Are you going?"

"Well, Daddy we just made it down here and we have hurricanes coming left and right. I just don't think we can afford to drive back up to Kentucky. I'm sorry," I apologized. "I'll call and send flowers. Do you want me to put your name on our flowers?"

"Yeah, can you do that? That would be great," he said.

I called Daddy later to see how he was doing. I couldn't tell if he was in mourning because the tone of his voice was so bland. It was the same voice he used when Mildred died.

As Bill and I got settled into our new home and became accustomed to our surroundings, I knew we'd made the right decision to move. I still called Daddy every single day. Our conversations were repetitive and sometimes just plain stupid. I didn't know if I was doing it out of some weird responsibility or that I loved him. It was such fine line between love and hate.

In 2005, Daddy flew to Florida to participate in his new great grandson's birthday and Baptism. He had not been on a plane since World War II. Donnie paid for his first class accommodations. Our visit was like a fairytale, with four generations together in the same room. Although having difficulty in walking due to two knee replacements, Daddy's general health was good.

Soon after he returned to Oklahoma, Wilma took a turn for the worse. Having been ill for several years, Daddy finally made the decision to place her in a nursing home. With all the medication she took, he was unable to keep up with the schedule. He said he caught her taking medication that she had already taken a few hours earlier. He felt devastated as now he was alone in his house after more than thirty years of marriage. I still called him every day. His voice, although upbeat at times, also echoed a sense of sadness. Occasionally, he asked if I felt sorry for him. My response was "No," although I hated myself for that. I planned a trip to New York to visit one of my cousins and his wife in June.

I was surprised by Daddy's reaction to my trip to the Big Apple when I told him. "Now don't forget that I'm going to New York," I said. "I'll be up there for a week. If anything happens, will you please call me? I'll have a cell phone so I will try to call you every day."

"That's fine," he said. "You go on, have a good time. You know I was stationed in Long Island during the Army. I use to take the ferry across and hit the bars every night. Now you be careful up there. Don't take a taxi and for heaven sakes, don't ride the subway. And don't walk on those streets by yourself and never at night. Don't speak to anyone."

"Well, Daddy, how in the world am I going to go anywhere? Don't worry about me. Take care of yourself and Wilma," I said.

The morning after I arrived in Manhattan, Daddy called. "Susan, she passed away. The funeral is in a few days. You told me to call you if something happened," he said.

"Daddy, I'm so sorry," I said. "Are you all right?"

"Yeah, I'm okay. Don't even think you are coming out here. I mean you don't need to come out here and then turn around and go back," he said. "If you want to come, why don't you come later?"

"Are you sure you'll be okay?" I worried.

"Sure," he answered. "Don't worry about me. You have a good time."

The entire week I spent in New York was overshadowed with the guilt of not going to the funeral. Maybe it was because Wilma had been so good to Daddy and I really loved her for that. Or maybe it was because Daddy sounded so lost. He called after the funeral, letting me know that he was sitting in his recliner alone in his house. That really raised the guilt meter.

Within a few weeks, Daddy announced that he had sold his house and was moving into an independent living facility in Vinita, Oklahoma. He gave a logical assessment of his situation, stating that living out in the country by the lake in the winter time would not be reasonable since he was alone. The electricity fails from so much ice and snow; and the nearest hospital is more than twenty miles away. I, then, realized that he was truly afraid.

I made the trip to Oklahoma by plane, alone. With the help of Daddy's friends, he sold and gave away a lot of his furniture. He called a moving truck to take what was left of his furniture and clothing to his new apartment in the independent living facility. A couple of close friends, Mary and her husband, Fred, also helped him set up housekeeping in his new place. It was a nice apartment with a lot of amenities, including cable television. Living out on the lake, Daddy only had a roof antenna. He boasted proudly of his decisions, confident that he would be safe even in the dreaded winters of Oklahoma. I stayed a few more days, going through his papers, setting up a filing system for his bills, making necessary phone calls, and filling out forms to settle his wife's estate. I was better at that than moving furniture. The day before I left, we went to the cemetery where his aunt, uncle, cousin, and now his beloved Wilma was buried. I wanted to ask him so many questions but I could see there was a sorrowful look in his eyes.

"You know, Susan, you are the only one I have left," he said, staring at the grave markers.

"Now, Daddy, that isn't true. You've got your grandson and great-grandson . . . and don't forget Bill," I replied.

"Yeah, but my grandson has his own life, his own family. You're the only close blood kin I have left. Don't you die on me," he said, jokingly.

"Well, I'll try not to," I answered. "I have no plans of that nature."

It was no use trying to pry difficult words out of him since it was obvious there was more to his life, his story, than I ever knew. I left the next day with so much hurt, so much confusion, but with a renewed appreciation of my life back in Florida.

As my calls resumed each day, Daddy seemed to adapt to his new surroundings easily. His dear friend, Mary, who had taken care of the housework at the old house for years, still continued to come once a week to clean his apartment, wash his clothes, and buy groceries. I was so grateful for her loyalty, often telling Daddy how lucky he was to have her.

In May 2007, during one phone call, I mentioned to Daddy that I wanted to write down some history of the days back in the 1920s and '30s.

"Why in the world would you want to know about that?" he asked.

"Because I think it's interesting and the fact is if those stories aren't written down, then that part of history will be lost forever. So will you do it?" I asked. "The next time I'll bring my laptop and as you talk I can just type away."

"What is it that you want to know?" he asked, cautiously.

"I want to know about your people, how they lived, what you did when you were a little boy . . . about the good times and the hard times," I answered. "I want to know everything."

After telling me that he thought I was crazy and wasting my time, I thanked him with a reminder of holding him to his promise. I don't think he believed me until I called the following week to say we were coming to visit. "Daddy, get ready with the stories!"

We drove to Missouri and spent the night in a motel. We avoided as many interstate highways as possible, enjoying the rolling hills, horse and cattle farms, and lack of heavy traffic. Daddy was thrilled to see us, doting over us like we were celebrities, showing us off to some of the residents. I felt embarrassed but he was having such a good time. Because he had some difficulty breathing, we planned one event each day. We went to Walmart one day. The next day we went to Sonic, his favorite place to eat. Then we drove around to different little towns listening to Daddy's speech on the history of the area. One day we visited the Will Rogers Museum although we cut it short when Daddy seemed very tired. I got the idea that he didn't get out of his apartment very much. At eighty-eight years old, he appeared in reasonably good health and with a positive attitude. Still overweight, it didn't impair his ability to move around with some assistance. His mind was sharp, his memory better than most folks half his age.

One late afternoon, Bill had already gone to the visitor's apartment we were staying in at the same facility. I could tell that Daddy wanted to talk.

"Susan, I think I'm going to sell my car. I don't really need it. Mary gets my groceries. The local pharmacy delivers my medicine. A friend of mine comes here to cut my hair. The hospital and my doctor are right next door. I don't have a reason to keep that car. I could save a lot of money not having the upkeep. The car insurance is out of sight," he explained.

"Well, if that is what you want to do, I think that's fine. Now, if you want to keep it for a while, that's okay too. Whatever you want. I know you love your car," I said. "Just be sure."

"I've got a friend at a dealership that's going to help me sell it. I told him anything over the amount we agreed on, he could keep. I think that's only fair," he explained.

"That sounds good to me," I said.

"I just wanted to run that by you," he said. "I really don't need a car. I mean, there's no place for me to go. I've gotten everything and everybody coming here for me, even the hearing aid man."

"Now there's another thing I want to talk to you about. I want us to go to church tomorrow. The Holy Ghost Catholic Church is not even a mile from here. It's that tan brick church on the corner on the left going out of town. That is where your mother and I were baptized into the Catholic faith, the same church. I want us to go to Mass. Will you take me?" he asked.

I was so shocked, my heart ached. "Of course, we'll go," I said. "I would love to go."

"Good, I was hoping you'd say yes," he said. "I know you're tired because I sure am. I'm going to bed soon. Why don't you go on and get some rest? Mass is at nine. I'll be ready. Don't knock, just come on in."

I kissed my father on the forehead and went to the apartment anxious to tell Bill all the news. He, too, thought it was a good idea to sell the car, saying that between sitting in the blazing sun, not being driven much, and the harsh winters, the value would only depreciate.

"Susan, I think that you and your Daddy should go to Mass. I'll stay here, no problem. I think it is a father daughter thing," my husband wisely said.

I laughed. "You know, sometimes you just amaze me. When did you get so smart?" I joked.

I picked Daddy up at eight thirty on Sunday morning. He was already dressed and ready when I walked into his apartment. He said he had been up for hours and I believed him. He was so excited. He handed me the keys and I bravely drove his big car to church.

"Susan, don't take this the wrong way but since your mother and Wilma are gone, do you think I could get back in good graces with the Catholic church?" he asked, timidly.

"I don't see why not. I'll check it out for you if you want me to," I said.

"Would you do that for me?" he asked.

"Sure. Let's get inside now. Don't want to be late. Watch the roof in case it falls in," I said.

During the Mass, I didn't hear a word the priest said. I went through the motions but my mind was so overwhelmed by just being with my father in church, that I could hardly keep composure. I knew that God was blessing us in so many ways. I thanked Him. I wondered if my mother's spirit was nearby. I thought I saw a tear in my father's eyes.

After church I asked Daddy if he was ready to tell me some stories. He seemed a little anxious but very willing. So that afternoon, Daddy and Bill joked, laughing for more than an hour while I set up my laptop, wrote some questions to ask, and prepared to type away. Then my husband excused himself as he knew that Daddy wouldn't get serious if he stayed.

"Daddy, are you ready?" I asked,

"Sure, what do you want to know?" he asked.

"All about you!" I replied.

CHAPTER FOURTEEN

Daddy tilted his head like he didn't hear me well. "What do you mean? I thought you wanted stories about Harlan," he said, leaning back in his recliner.

"I do. I want to know about how it was like when you were a little boy growing up in Harlan," I said, hoping he would finally open up about his life.

"Aww, you don't want to know about that stuff," he said, shaking his head.

"Yes, I do. I really do!" I said. "You just talk and I'll type."

"Well, what do you want to know?" he asked, frowning as if he wanted to change his mind.

"Oh, good grief, Daddy, tell me what happened that your mother ended up in Detroit. Tell me how in the world you ended up in Vinita," I said in frustration. "I really want to know."

"I've never talked about it before. Are you sure you want to hear this?" he asked. "Some of it I remember and some of it my mother told me. My daddy never told me what really happened. I mean he never told me to hate my mother, he just never said anything."

"Daddy, take a deep breath and start talking," I joked. "If you get tired, we'll take a break."

We laughed. It was awkward, sitting with my father, prying into his private life as if I was a stranger. In a small way, I guess I was. I was very acquainted with the raging violent drunk. I was still getting to know the man in the present and accept his sobriety. Now, I was going to be allowed to enter his past. Little did I know how his childhood ruled his adulthood, affecting his life and those closest to him.

Daddy began, "When I was very little, about four or five years old, my parents and I lived right in the city of Harlan. My father owned a grocery store, and he worked all the time. According to my mother, she said some of Daddy's brothers didn't like her and set her up. Someone told the city police that a young man by the name of Chester Pike, a taxi driver, was in our apartment with my mother and me. Uncle Harmon, one of Daddy's brothers, was Chief of Police at the time. Anyway, the police came to our apartment and made the man leave. The police were witnesses that Chester Pike was in our apartment without my Daddy being there."

"So what happened when you father found out?" I asked.

"Daddy filed for divorce. Back then, the judge was a friend of the Noe family. During the divorce proceeding, the judge awarded me to my Daddy. When all that was going on, Daddy took me to a cousin's house in Fairview to live until it was over. Then when he came to get me, he simply told me that my mother would not be back. That was it. My mother was gone," he said. There was a long uncomfortable pause. I stared at my laptop and shuffled some papers, avoiding eye contact. I felt like he needed that.

"It seemed that the judge ordered my mother never see me or come back into Harlan County without my Daddy's permission. After the trial, my mother went to Pineville, Kentucky, where Mr. Pike lived. Later they moved to Detroit, I don't know why but it seems that she had a sister up there at the time. I can't say for sure. There's no record of them getting married because when she married Hugo, that marriage license shows that my father is the only other marriage. After that, Daddy and I moved in with George, another brother of Daddy's, Aunt Ella, and

151

their daughter, Mildred. From what I was told, Uncle George decided to go to Vinita, Oklahoma to open up a barber shop. Some of Aunt Ella's kinfolk lived there. So when George told my father about his plans, George also suggested that I go live with them in Vinita. My Daddy realized that when they left, he wouldn't have a place or no one to care for me while he worked. I know my father loved me. At first, he didn't want me to go but he decided it was best. George went on to Vinita in the car while Aunt Ella, cousin Mildred, and I stayed in Harlan until Mildred graduated from Harlan High School. Then we packed up and got on the train heading out west. Before we left, somehow Aunt Ella got in contact with my mother who was still in Pineville at the time with that Pike man. When the train made its regular stop there, my mother was at the depot. I hugged her so hard. I hadn't seen her since before the divorce. I missed her so much. Aunt Ella always told me to love my mother and I did. Oh God, I hated to get back on that train," Daddy cried, wiping his eyes.

"Daddy, I had no idea," I said. "You were just a little boy."

Quickly, his demeanor changed. "I got used to it. Aunt Ella was good to me," he boasted. "Their house was small, just two bedrooms. Mildred got a scholarship so she was away at college by then. I really missed her. Since she was a few years older than me, she was always taking care of me, and picking on me at the same time. I think she loved me more than anybody. Aunt Ella's sister came to live with us so they fixed my bedroom out on the sleeping porch, which you would call a screened in porch. I had a cot on the south end of the porch up against the wall. During the warm months, George and Ella set up a small bed and slept out on the porch with me. After they got rained on a few times, they hung a canvas up to try to keep the water from soaking the bed. Then in the winter months, I slept on my cot underneath the dining room table. I didn't mind. Being a well-educated little woman, Aunt Ella loved to read books. I remember her reading the Bible from cover to cover many times. She was a devoted Southern Baptist, always wearing high-collared long dresses with long sleeves and big bloomers. I never knew of her using makeup or going to a dance. Sometimes she took me to the show on the chance that she would win some new dishes. The theater would have a drawing to win different things. I loved the movies. She always took me places as long as I behaved like a little gentleman. There was a cannery in Vinita and when it was time to can green beans, she took me there to help her snap beans. I got really good at breaking beans. We got a quarter for every basket of beans we snapped. That money helped with my school clothes. Sometimes when Aunt Ella gave me her spare change, I sneaked and bought Bull Durham chewing tobacco. In the winter, I got a pair of boots. In the summer, I wore old shoes or went barefooted."

Daddy took a drink of ice water, cleared his throat, and continued, "Aunt Ella was a good mother to me. She read the Bible to me every day. I don't know how many times she read the Good Book all the way through but I know it's plenty. When I was bad, she whipped me with the punch stick."

"Daddy, what's a punch stick?" I asked.

"That's a big stick, like the end of a broom handle, that she used to punch the clothes to wash them on the stove," he explained. "When she washed clothes, she put a wash tub on top of the stove and boiled water, then add the clothes. She would take the stick to punch the clothes, swishing them. I could tell she cared about me, that she really loved me . . . when she hit me."

"Really," I said, trying not to judge his warped sense of affection. "What about Uncle George?"

"Uncle George didn't like children. I mean he loved his daughter and I think he liked me but he never showed it much. When I was little he told me I was going to end up in jail all the time. He was a lonesome man. He could sit out on the porch for hours, not moving a muscle, just thinking about stuff, I guess. He always dressed well with a suit and tie. He was a 32nd Degree Mason. He wore a cowboy hat, smoked cigars, and liked his bourbon. He never drank in the house. I guess Aunt Ella would have had a fit. He never took me anywhere and hardly ever was home. He owned four barber shops at one time. He's the one who talked me into being a barber after the war," he said. "Daddy wanted me to be a doctor. My cousin, Guy Noe, was supposed to be a doctor but he settled for being a pharmacist at Green Mill Drug Store."

"When did you see your Daddy when you were so very young?" I asked. "I mean Kentucky is a long way from Oklahoma."

"In the summertime, Aunt Ella fixed me a box of fried chicken, pinned money on my underwear, tagged me, and handed me over to the conductor on the Frisco Railroad. I was very young at the time. The best I can remember, the trip took two days and two nights in a pullman coach, a sleeping car. I changed trains and conductors in St. Louis and in Louisville. The conductors saw that I was fed. I got to eat in the dining car. When I arrived at the Harlan Depot, my daddy was waiting on me. I did this every summer. Sometimes I rode the bus but I enjoyed riding the train more," he added.

"Did your mother ever come to Harlan when you were little or get in contact with you?" I asked.

"No, not that I can remember," he answered. "Maybe she was afraid or maybe she thought it was useless, being that the Noes had so much influence in Harlan at the time. Then again, it could be she just didn't want to. I don't know."

"When did you see her?" I asked, cautiously.

"Well, when Jewell and I got married, we went to Detroit for a visit. I have a picture of the three of us. I am in my Army uniform. Also when you were born, my mother sneaked into Harlan to see you. She held you in her arms. Of course, you don't remember that. Then when I married Wilma, we made a visit up morth. In her later years, my mother and Hugo decided to move to Somerset, Kentucky, back to her hometown and her kinfolk," he said.

"You really didn't spend any time with her growing up, I guess," I said. "Did you like spending summers in Harlan?"

"Yeah, I had the run of the town. Daddy worked all the time. He had grocery stores and then when Harlan became a wet territory, he opened a couple of liquor stores. He had a black woman to clean and take care of me in his apartment during the day. The only thing she refused to do was cook for me. Sometimes she let me come to her house over in Georgetown where the blacks lived and ate good home-cooking with her family. But most of the time, I ate at the cafes or drug stores and put it on Daddy's tab. We ate all our meals out. In the evenings, I went to the movies since my Aunt Margie owned the theater. I really liked Wallace's Confectionary. Some of the diners stayed open late in town so I sat in there a lot. I ate some of the best food at a boarding house across from Robert's Motor. I can't remember the name of it," he said. "I was on my own most of the time."

"I went to four high schools in four years, I was expelled from two of them. My senior year was at Claremore, Oklahoma where my cousin Mildred was teaching at the time. I didn't finish, though, leaving a few weeks before graduation. Aunt Ella received a phone call from someone in Harlan saying that my father was about to die. So I left school, hitchhiked to Harlan, thinking I was going to bury my father when I got there. I don't remember what his sickness was but he recovered completely. Later while I was in the Army, my captain wrote a letter to the Claremore school. He requested that I be allowed to graduate due to the circumstances and the fact that I hadn't failed any classes. I got my diploma. I was so proud."

I had to ask him the burning question, prepared for a complete shutdown or banishment. I just blurted it out, "Daddy, why did you drink so much?"

Daddy let out a big sigh and said, "In the beginning, it was so it wouldn't hurt so much. Later, on, it was because I liked it."

Seeing signs of exhaustion in his face, I decided to stop the interview. "Well, I think we've done enough damage for today. Why don't we stop right here? Tomorrow, maybe you can think of some of the pranks you pulled or the trouble you got into when you were a kid," I suggested.

He agreed. It proved to be the most important conversation with my father I ever had or will have. I felt as though I was just introduced to a child-like man. With his distorted sense of love, combined with the emotional and physical abandonment of family, he turned his reality into fantasy. The liquor eased the pain while rationalizing the violence.

The next day, I continued to collect some tales, some true, some questionable, but all from the mind of a man who seemed to survive by placing a positive spin on the most tragic circumstances and avoiding a painful past.

"I want you to know that I'm going to write a story about you," I said.

"You are? I don't know if you should do that," he said. "You know there's some of those things I told you that you can't tell."

I attempted to ease his mind about my knowledge of his life in Lexington which he had sworn me to secrecy. "I know that. I won't write about your involvement with the crime families in the Lexington Mafia or that fiasco in Covington, Kentucky. I'm just going to write about your childhood, our family, and some of the history of Harlan," I said.

"If you're hell bent on doing this, then you've got to promise me something," he insisted.

"You can't write about this stuff until I'm dead and buried."

"Well, Daddy, that will be never. You're never going to die," I joked, half serious.

"My mother was a hundred and four when she closed her eyes for the last time and I plan on beating that number. You have a long time to wait," he warned.

I felt sad leaving my father to return to Florida. He never showed any emotion when we left but now I understood why. He was a master of hiding.

I contacted the local priest in Vinita, explained the situation, and asked him to visit Daddy for confession and communion. At the end of the week, Daddy called.

"Well, you did it. The priest came and took my confession. You won't believe it, but after he absolved me, it cracked off the biggest thunder you ever heard," he said.

"Daddy, you're joking!" I said.

"No, I'm telling the truth. To beat it all, it was sunny outside," he said. "That priest looked at me and I looked at him. We laughed. After he gave me communion, he left pretty quick. Maybe I scared him."

"You probably did. Or maybe my mother had something to do with it!" I warned.

In July, Daddy threw me another ball of surprise. He called to tell me that he had gotten a card in the mail from the local funeral home advertising for pre-paid funerals. After a scheduled appointment in which they came to his apartment, he signed on the dotted line and arranged for payment.

"Daddy, are you sick?" I asked, wondering if he was telling me the whole truth.

"No, I'm not sick. I'm just fine. I've been thinking about it for a long time. That is what Mildred did and it was so easy for me when she died. I just don't want to leave you with a mess," he said. "You'll thank me."

"Oh yeah, it was easy for you. Heck, you didn't waste any time, had her in the ground before she was cold. You do what you think is best," I said. "If this makes you feel better, then that's fine."

For the next couple of months, I noticed during our phone conversations a change in my father's voice, a slowness in his responses and a lack of the customary banter. In October, he became ill and spent a few days in the hospital. After a second visit to the hospital, it was apparent that he would not be returning to his apartment. I flew out there to help him ease into the transition of entering a nursing home. Once again, Mary and Fred helped move what furniture he wanted to take with him. With a rented car, I helped with the smaller things that Daddy wanted to keep. I arranged his room and made sure that he had a television. In talking with his doctor, it was my understanding that his health would improve but not to the point of being self sufficient. The last day I was there, he joked as usual, avoiding the reality of living out the rest of his life in that room. He threw out orders on how and where to hang his pictures, the correct angle of his television, the arrangement of his clothing, and the importance of the remote control, all from his bed.

As the late afternoon sunlight shone through his only window, a sadness crept into his room. "You know, Susan, I didn't think I would have ended up in here. I really wanted you and me to go together," he said.

"What do you mean?" I asked, confused by his words.

"I always thought it would have been nice if we died together," he said. "I'm afraid that when I die, you mother will be up there with Saint Peter at the Gates of Heaven and she'll tell him not to let me in. I figured if you go with me, I've got somebody on my side."

"Daddy, I'm sorry but I have no intentions of leaving this earth right now," I said, not knowing if he was serious or joking. "Besides, you're not going anywhere, remember?"

"Well, when I die, you'll be well taken care of," he whispered. "The nursing home isn't going to get my money."

"Daddy, don't you know that I love you anyway. Why do you say things like that?" I asked.

"I thought you'd love me more if I had money," he said, looking away from me.

"That's stupid. I don't care about your money. I'd be in a poor shape if I did," I quipped. "I love you."

"You're going to go now, aren't you?" he asked, a hint of fear in his voice.

"Yes, I have to pack my bag for tomorrow's flight. Mary is picking me up at your apartment and taking me back to Tulsa to catch the plane. You should have a phone in your room some-time tomorrow. I will call you when I get home. If something happens that you don't have a phone, I'll call the nurses station and they can tell you."

"You won't be back?" he asked.

"No, Daddy, the flight is very early. Mary's picking me up around four in the morning," I explained. I felt like I was hug-ging my father for the last time. "I love you. I really do."

"I love you too," he said, waving his hand as I walked out of his room.

I sat in the rented car in front of the nursing home for what seemed like a long time. Every time I thought my tears stopped, I broke down again. I did love my Daddy. He was a sad pathetic old man who continued to struggle with the idea that he was not worthy of anyone's love. In my heart, I forgave him, know-ing that he could never accept the painful life he gave my mother and me.

On November seventeenth, my father passed away. As Bill, Donnie, and I sat in the front row of the funeral home in Vinta, Oklahoma, a rush of emotions from the last few months over-whelmed me. Outside, a wild wind stirred the leaves. The hot sun shone boldly, like a summer's day. I looked around at the handful of people who came to pay their last respects. The priest said a few kind words. Bill sat beside me, my son behind me. Wilma's children occupied a seat along with Mary. The room was nearly empty. Several floral arrangements were placed around the casket. A beautiful spray of flowers draped over one end of the open casket. I had Daddy dressed in his dark blue suit, white shirt, and tie. He had lost nearly one hundred pounds in two weeks after I had left him the last time. I hardly recognized him. After the short service, we rode in a limousine, following the hearse to the cemetery. Sitting in the folding chairs under the funeral tent beside my father's open grave, the fierce wind stirred so violently that the attendants had to hold the tent poles in place.

Mary leaned over to me and whispered, "Look at this wind! You know, I think your Daddy is up to his old pranks, just to let us know his spirit is nearby."

"I believe you're right," I answered, muffling a slight giggle.

As I watched clusters of beautiful flowers swirl away with the wind, I realized that all the years I clung to hatred only colored my soul, that forgiveness was for everybody . . . including myself. It was time to let go.

Domestic Abuse and Alcoholism Resource Help Information

NDVH (National Domestic Violence Hotline)
1-800-799-7233
1-800-787-3224 TTY line
http://ndvh.org

NTDAH (National Teen Dating Abuse Helpline)
1-866-331-9474
1-866-331-8453 TTY line
http://loveisrespect.org

ACA WSO (Adult Children of Alcoholics World Service Organization)
PO Box 3216
Torrance, Ca. 90510   Phone: 310-534-1815
www.adultchildren.org
Email message only: info@adultchildren.org

Al-Anon Family Group Headquarters, Inc.
1600 Corporate Landing Parkway
Virginia Beach, Va. 23454-5617
Tel: 757-563-1600
Fax: 757-563-1655
wso@al-anon.org
You can also call 1-800-4AL-ANON (1-888-425-2666)
Mon.–Fri., 8am–6pm ET for meeting info

National Network to End Domestic Violence
2001 S. Street, NW, Suite 400, Washington, D.C. 20009
www.nnedv.org

WomenLaw
55 Washington St., Suite 614
Brooklyn, N.Y. 11201
Fax: 718-534-7412
www.womenslaw.org

Please contact us for any reason. You may choose to receive your response through email or by signing in to our secure website.

About the Author

To Hide the Truth is the second book written by Susan Noe Harmon, a native of Harlan County, Kentucky. Her first novel, *Under the Weeping Willow*, garnered successful reviews as an Appalachian story rich in history and family values. Harmon has also written several short stories which are included in *The Zinnia Tales*, *Self-Rising Flowers*, and *Christmas Blooms*, all published by Mountain Girl Press. Recently, her short story, "Jake's Cove," was published by MtnValy Publishing, in the anthology *Zeniths & Zephyrs*.

Retired from Kentucky State Government, Susan and her husband, Bill, live in Zephyrhills, Florida. Having a passion for writing, she turned a hobby into a second career; beginning with a five hundred word short story about Christmas, published in the *Zephyrhills News* in 2005. Harmon is a member of the Third Tuesday Writer's Group and the Florida Writer's Association.

To learn more about the author, please visit her website www.snharmon.com .

Her novels and shorts stories are available for order on her website. If requested, she will be happy to sign a copy for you or as a gift for a friend.

Susan Noe Harmon is available for book talks, readings, and signings. You may contact her at snharmon11@yahoo.com for information about an appearance.

The cover for *To Hide the Truth* was created by

**GAINOR
ROBERTS**

34730 Sturgeon Loop
Zephyrhills, FL 33541
813 469-1641
website: www.gainor.biz
email: gainor@tampabay.rr.com

Gainor Roberts moved to Zephyrhills in 2001 from Rhode Island where she taught painting classes and had a gallery in the small town of Westerly. Art has been a passion with Gainor for most of her life, and she can remember drawing pictures as a toddler and feigning illness to stay home from school and draw pictures all day.

She considers herself a realist painter and has been greatly influenced by the Impressionists. She studied painting at the Art Students' League, in New York, with Robert Brackman and later at the National Academy of Design and Lyme Academy of Fine arts, studying painting, drawing and sculpture. Her paintings are characterized by her love affair with color and design, and she frequently uses fruits and vegetables as subject matter, although she loves to paint a wide variety of subject matter, including portraits of people and animals.

Her mediums are oil, watercolor, pastel, egg tempera, monotype and various drawing mediums. Her love of art is reflected by a love of traditional artist materials and techniques although she is familiar with and has great affection for many contemporary artists and their mediums. Her subjects are still life, landscape, symbolic still life paintings, and portraits. She teaches painting and computer classes at Carrollwood Cultural Center and occasionally she works with students privately as well. She has exhibited her work widely in New England and more recently in the Tampa Bay area and has had several solo shows: 50-year Retrospective of her work in the fall of 2005 at Horizon Line Gallery in Temple Terrace, and a solo show at her alma mater in Elmira, New York during the summer of 2008.

She is a member of many art organizations including the Egg Tempera Society, the American Impressionist Society, The Society of Exhibiting Artists, TESA (past secretary of the board of directors) Monotype Guild of New England (honorary member), North Tampa Arts League, Florida Plein Air Society, The Florida Committee of the National Museum of Women in the Arts, The National League of American Pen Women (Art Member), and Les Girls Painting Society.

Her paintings and portraits are in numerous private collections.

To order more Mountain Girl Press titles
Go to **http://www.mountaingirlpress.com**

Join author Tammy Robinson Smith for a literary treat for all ages, *Emmybeth Speaks*.

Emmybeth Johnson is a nine year old girl who lives in Little Creek, Tennessee in the foothills of the Appalachian Mountains. Her story begins late in the summer of 1971. Emmybeth likes to know what is happening with the adults in her life and in the community in general. She has a favorite "hidey hole" where she can listen as her mother, grandmother and the ladies from her church's sewing circle discuss the latest news and gossip from Little Creek. Emmybeth treats the reader to the "goings on" of the community from her naïve perspective, which is sometimes closer to the truth than she knows!

⚜

Visit the hills and hollers of Kentucky as Susan Noe Harmon explores the lives of three generations of Appalachian women in her first novel, *Under the Weeping Willow*.

Step into the lives of one Kentucky family who will capture your heart and leave you wanting more. Belle, Pearl and Sara, three generations of Appalachian women will teach you about life in a 1950's family and how it touched the future. *Under the Weeping Willow* is a story about the closeness of family and how they enjoy the good times and pull together through the bad. Come into their world and live and learn from it along with them. You will feel like you've found a home and a family of Kentucky kin.

⚜

Come along from past to present day Northeast Tennessee with Elizabeth Barker for her Mountain Girl Press debut novel, *Journey of the Brass Bed*.

Follow the journey of an antique brass bed as it is passed from family to family with no one learning its secret. Sometimes the very thing that can save you is right in front of you. Your heart's desires are often as close as your bedpost. Clever writing, interesting characters, and a fresh plot unfold and keep you reading for hours. Come along for the journey which will ultimately lead you home.

❧❦❧

Enter the world of Appalachian women and see what happens when struggles are faced and overcome.

The stories depicted in *The Zinnia Tales*, *Self-Rising Flowers*, and *Christmas Blooms* will take you to a place where strong women survive. Each short story collection is filled with stories that celebrate what it means to be an "Appalachian woman." Each collection will strike a note with anyone who has ever called the mountains home, or just wishes she lives there. Readers will delight in the warmth of these tales, which demonstrate the richness of the place where these women live their lives, and tell their stories. Fiction about women, written by women, these rich works exemplify the Mountain Girl Press mission statement: Stories that celebrate the wit, humor and strength of Appalachian women.

❧❦❧

Take a trip to Coleman, Virginia where pie is not the only dish served!

Mountain Girl Press author Lisa Hall takes a humorous, yet thoughtful look at the life in a fictional small Appalachian town.

Her "Cutie Pies" series keeps heartwarming humor on the front burner!

Secrets, Lies, and Pies

In Coleman, Virginia, one can expect a generous helping of humiliated beauty queens, ex-jocks, outlaws, and Marlene Prescotts's legendary pie. Marlene is the beautiful and successful owner of a bakery called Cutie Pies. When the Coleman Canasta Club, better know as The Hens, set out to destroy Marlene's reputation with a malicious rumor, Marlene and her two best friends cook up the perfect plan to gain sweet revenge! *Secrets, Lies, and Pies* is the first in the Coleman, Virginia series.

Cheaters, Pies, and Lullabies

Return to Coleman for *Cheaters, Pies, and Lullabies*, the much anticipated sequel to *Secrets, Lies, and Pies*. Nothing that anyone does in this small town goes without notice. So, how long can cheating spouses commence to carrying on without being caught? How does a new mother cope with evil stares and nasty comments as her parenting skills come under attack? Readers will find the answers to these and many other questions in *Cheaters, Pies, and Lullabies*.

Coming Thanksgiving weekend 2009, the sequel that will make the "Cutie Pies," series a trilogy!

Play Dates, Pies, and Sad Goodbyes

The end of *Cheaters, Pies, and Lullabies* left readers with lots of questions, and found some of the ladies in Coleman at a crossroads. Is Charity's marriage worth saving? Will Marlene sell Cutie Pies in order to stay home with her son?

Some life-changing decisions, a devastating diagnosis, and a family tragedy will forever change the lives of Marlene, Allison, Dorothy and Charity. If you are a fan of the "Cutie Pies," series, do not miss this opportunity to know the characters like never before.

A bit of sour, a dusting of sugar, and a sprinkling of tears will make the third book of the "Cutie Pies," series more tempting than a big ole' slice of Marlene's pie. You will want to dig in! Come back to Coleman for *Play Dates, Pies, and Sad Goodbyes*!

www.ingramcontent.com/pod-product-compliance
Lightning Source LLC
Chambersburg PA
CBHW030014290326
41934CB00005B/333